REDEFINING RETIREMENT:

CREATING
SECURITY IN AN
UNSECURE WORLD

REDEFINING RETIREMENT:

CREATING **SECURITY** IN AN **UNSECURE** WORLD

CHRISTOPHER K. ABTS

Advantage®

Published by Advantage, Charleston, South Carolina.
Member of Advantage Media Group.

ADVANTAGE is a registered trademark and the Advantage colophon is a trademark of Advantage Media Group, Inc.

Printed in the United States of America.

ISBN: 978-159932-338-1
LCCN: 2013940315

This publication is designed to provide accurate and authoritative information in regard to the subject matter covered. It is sold with the understanding that the publisher is not engaged in rendering legal, accounting, or other professional services. If legal advice or other expert assistance is required, the services of a competent professional person should be sought.

Advantage Media Group is proud to be a part of the Tree Neutral® program. Tree Neutral offsets the number of trees consumed in the production and printing of this book by taking proactive steps such as planting trees in direct proportion to the number of trees used to print books. To learn more about Tree Neutral, please visit **www.treeneutral.com**. To learn more about Advantage's commitment to being a responsible steward of the environment, please visit **www.advantagefamily.com/green**

Advantage Media Group is a publisher of business, self-improvement, and professional development books and online learning. We help entrepreneurs, business leaders, and professionals share their Stories, Passion, and Knowledge to help others Learn & Grow. Do you have a manuscript or book idea that you would like us to consider for publishing? Please visit **advantagefamily.com** or call **1.866.775.1696**.

To Julia, my wife, soul mate and best friend. Thank you for your constant encouragement, support and wisdom. You are my inspiration.

To our three beautiful children, Kendelle, Henry and Spencer, the world is your canvas, the colors are your dreams. Make your life a beautiful painting.

To the hundreds of retirees I have had the honor to help over the past 20 years, thank you for your trust and for the opportunity to serve you and your families.

CONTENTS

On the Path to Prosperity

My father was a financial advisor, and his father worked in the financial services industry as well, during the Great Depression, no less. Times have certainly changed over the years, but the idea of helping people create, grow, and protect their savings has deep roots in my family.

As I was growing up, sometimes I would meet people with whom my dad or grandpa had worked. They always seemed so appreciative, and I was proud of that. I liked the idea of helping people pursue their dreams.

It's no secret that much has changed since my forebears plied their trade. Company-sponsored pensions, once a retirement staple, are all but gone, replaced by the largely self-funded 401(k)s and IRAs. Government programs such as Social Security and Medicare are severely underfunded, raising questions about their viability in the future. Investments once considered "safe"—mutual funds, for example—have proved to be anything but.

Tax laws change so often and are so complicated that the average person could not be expected to keep up with them. It's the same with the thousands of investment options available today, with prospectuses so long and unintelligible that reading them is all but pointless.

All of this is compounded by an uncertain economic environment, extended market volatility, and some contemptible investment professionals who have given the entire industry a black eye. It's no wonder so many people are drowning in a sea of questions rather than planning and living a safe, secure, and comfortable retirement.

This book will help answer many of the questions you may be facing. Like my father and grandfather before me, I am dedicated to helping you understand the many variables that can directly affect your financial future so that you can indeed make your retirement dreams come true.

What that retirement looks like has changed dramatically in those three generations, from the early days of the last century until today. People have far different expectations of what those years will be like. When my father was a financial advisor, the "three-legged stool" was a standard of retirement planning. The legs represented the three bulwarks of retirement finances, which were Social Security, a company pension, and your own savings and investments.

An advisor back then was simply helping clients to make the most of their savings and investments, allocating their portfolios to reduce risk and earn a fair rate of return. However, people were less dependent upon that money than they are today. Many people thought of that money as just something extra.

COLLAPSE OF THE THREE-LEGGED STOOL

That three-legged stool has changed forever. In fact, it is wobbly to the point of collapse. The only strong leg left is what retirees can do for themselves through their investments. A great many people have most of their savings in a retirement plan—a 401(k) or an IRA. What used to be just that something extra now makes up the bulk of a retiree's financial security.

As retirees live longer, they must find ways to make that money last. In effect, they now must create their own pension from their own assets, and they face a momentous challenge in learning how to do so. In many cases, they simply are not prepared.

They're facing a wide range of problems and uncertainties, not the least of which is dealing with the longevity that medical advances have made possible. The cost of health care has been increasing significantly faster than inflation. Medicare and Medicaid are in question, and retirees fear they cannot afford long-term-care insurance. They face an economy of low interest rates, a housing crisis, and unemployment. People often are being involuntarily forced into retiring early. The stock market went through what has been called a lost decade, with volatile swings that denied people the kind of returns they had been expecting. We're dealing with a significant amount of government debt.

REDEFINING RETIREMENT

In the face of those challenges, 78 million baby boomers are looking to retire, and if they are to succeed, they must redefine retirement. It's no longer a simple matter of a gold watch, a pension, and Social Security.

A few generations ago, they commonly moved in with the children. Grandpa and grandma lived at home. But relationships are far different today, with families often living on different coasts. It takes two wage earners to get by, in many cases, meaning that nobody can be home to offer care for elderly parents when that time comes. So grandma and grandpa need to make it on their own far longer than ever before—often, 25 years or more.

That's long enough that inflation, even at a conservative rate of 3 percent, can devastate their nest egg. Most retirees are not grasping the gravity of that situation. And often, at the end of that long stretch of retirement, they will need professional nursing care, and many have not prepared for that.

EARLY PLANNING IS ESSENTIAL

Years ago, my father, Henry W. Abts III, had some books on the New York Times best-selling list. One was called *The Living Trust*. He created one of the largest trust companies in the country. Earlier in my career I had an opportunity to work with him in his settlement department, helping people settle estates with a trust. I probably helped more people in a day than a typical estate planning attorney would settle in a year.

I learned that usually, after creating a trust, people would put it on the shelf, and the years would pass. The trust wouldn't protect them from market losses, or from inflation, or from the costs of a long-term illness. It wouldn't help them earn a fair rate of return, or assure them sufficient income. As a result, by the time the surviving spouse died, the estate usually was not large enough to need a trust anymore to settle it. Time had taken its toll on the estate. Mistakes were made, and money fell through the cracks. Estates, over time, dwindle.

I came to understand how to help people achieve their goals of financial security rather than see such losses time and time again. I learned that there was a better way. I knew that despite any market correction that might come our way, you can still earn a fair rate of return and be assured of a reasonable income that's adjusted for inflation. You can put the right plans in place for long-term financial security.

A TOUGH LESSON SELDOM TAUGHT

What I learned is that my industry does not often teach people that. The goals of so many in my industry are unfortunately not in line with the goals of the average investor, who is being fed a lot of false information, some of it intentionally. People are being harmed.

I recently met with a couple who in January of 2008 had a million dollars invested through a broker. They were taking out a reasonable amount of income. They had used the same broker for years as they accumulated money during their working lives. But before that couple came to see me, their broker had told them, "Now you only have $600,000. You need to reduce your income or sell your vacation home because you're going to run out of money." It was the broker's fault, not theirs, yet they had no recourse. They had been given bad advice.

The couple's CPA referred them to me to analyze why they were running out of money. When I ran the numbers for that couple, I explained that if they had followed our advice, they would probably have about $1.2 million. That's a difference of almost $600,000 that they lost because of bad advice. They were still operating as if they were in their accumulation years. They were taking too much market risk, and at the same time they were withdrawing money from those equities, even as the market plunged, and they were paying high fees. That's not an income plan.

Because they didn't know about a simple process, it cost them hundreds of thousands of dollars—and possibly their lifetime financial security. The root of their problem was that they were still with a broker who focused on the accumulation of assets. They had never made the move to an advisor who specializes in preservation. In fact, they were unaware that such advisors existed.

My job, my passion, is to teach people to understand the decisions they need to make and the things to watch out for so that they can avoid what happened to that couple. I tailor a plan that's unique to the individual. It's not a one-size-fits-all. The amount of risk that someone should take depends on the individual; it depends on the portfolio; and it depends on dreams and aspirations. That's why the plan must be custom designed.

A NEW STAGE OF LIFE

Most people would not attempt to climb Mount Everest on their own. Typically, climbers will look toward Sherpas, who have served as guides for generations in Nepal, high in the Himalayas. They help climbers prepare and show them along the routes that will get them to the top. They are seasoned and know every detail of the trails. But your guide is even more essential if you are to make it back down safely. Coming down the mountain can be the most perilous part. You're tired. Your defenses are down. You may very well fall at the critical moment. You need that guide.

As you approach retirement, you are moving to a different phase of life. You are descending the mountain. For years you have been climbing, in the accumulation phase of your life. Now you should be preparing to reap the benefits of all your hard work. Your stance now should be to preserve your life savings.

When people are in the accumulation phase, they're saving, they're growing, they're investing, they're taking that risk, and they're accumulating those assets. That might be in the form of a 401(k). They're adding to that 401(k) over those working years. When the market has a correction, they might not enjoy looking at their statements—maybe they don't even open them—but hopefully they're still adding to their retirement accounts. They still have an income, so they don't need to tap those savings. Those people will recover from a market drop much faster because they're not taking any money out and they're adding new money to the account, and possibly their employer is contributing to it in a match, as well.

Their experience is: "I saw a drop, but within a few years I was back to where I was, and more." They may come to expect the same in their retirement, but they will be in for a rude awakening. Not only will they be withdrawing from the account in retirement, but they will no longer be contributing to it. If the market dips, they will be in financial peril.

In retirement, people should move from accumulation to preservation. You must live off of what you've accumulated, and it must last your lifetime and your spouse's lifetime if you're married. The focus changes to preserving what you have and generating income off that money as efficiently as possible.

YOU NEED A PRESERVATION ADVISOR

That's when most people change advisors. Most advisors focus on accumulation. When the market corrects, they tell you to hang in there, the market will come back, wait it out. A retirement planning specialist, by contrast, focuses on retirement. You need qualified advice, and it must be specific to you. You cannot make a plan around the water cooler. What may have worked for your coworkers and friends and neighbors will not necessarily work for you.

If you do not change your investment strategy for retirement, you risk cracking the nest egg that you nurtured so long and losing much of it in a few years. Even if you had a million or more, you might have to go back to work against your will. It could be that bad. If during all your working years you saw the market bounce back after a correction, you may continue to think that's always the case. But if those bad years come early in your retirement, and while you are withdrawing money from your account for income, your portfolio is unlikely to ever bounce back, even if the Dow does. That can seem like a foreign concept to those who are still in the accumulation mode. They may refuse to believe it could happen to them, and they end up sadder but wiser. Millions of retirees who were in that situation in 2008 are nowhere near back to breakeven.

I will explain later in this book just how that startling scenario develops and the steps you can take to make sure it doesn't happen to you. You don't need to live in anxiety, watching every tick of the markets. With proper planning, you can move forward in comfort and certainty, no matter how the economic winds blow.

THE THREE BIG QUESTIONS

This book will help you answer three fundamental questions that you must address if you are to effectively plan for a fruitful retirement. I will deal with these in detail in later chapters: 1) Are you paying too much in taxes? 2) Is your level of risk appropriate? 3) Do you have a clear income plan for the rest of your life?

Are You Paying Too Much in Taxes?

I will help you examine whether you are missing opportunities to reduce your income tax and whether you are correctly taking advantage of tax deferral strategies. You need to review your tax return and make sure that you're using a productive look-forward approach. Have your advisors talked to you about tax-advantaged payoff strategies in which you can have about 85 to 90 percent of your income completely tax-free? Could that bring you into a lower tax bracket? Could that possibly reduce or eliminate tax on your Social Security?

We will take a look at the differences between traditional deferred-tax retirement accounts and the Roth IRAs in which you pay the tax up front, with the distribution tax-free. Have you perhaps been told that it doesn't make sense to convert your traditional retirement plan into a Roth IRA because you are in too high a tax bracket? Have you looked at ways to bring yourself into a lower tax bracket so possibly that might make sense? Maybe you're already in a low tax bracket and feeling that you don't need to do anything, but if that is the case, would it make sense to do a Roth conversion now? Have you examined the likelihood that your tax bracket and the tax rate will actually be higher in retirement, despite the oft-heard advice that the opposite will be true?

In this book, I will help you answer those questions. You need to think long term, not only for your own retirement but for your heirs as well. You want to avoid saddling them with a tax burden that could have been easily avoided.

Is Your Level of Risk Appropriate?

Is your risk exposure in line with your risk comfort level? If the market is doing well, and you're earning a fair rate of return, you may not be considering this. You're not concerned. Then along comes a correction in the market, and you panic. "I need to do something—and quick!" you tell yourself. Or you do nothing and just hang in there and learn firsthand how long it takes your portfolio to recover.

Now is the time to assess how much you could lose the next time the market has a correction. Rather than learning from sad experience, wouldn't it be better to go through a simple process to identify the scenario in advance and figure out how you would feel about it? In other words, wouldn't it be better to know your risk comfort level?

Do You Have a Clear Income Plan for the Rest of Your Life?

Almost all people approaching retirement agree upon the importance of an income plan, yet less than a third of them, according to one survey, actually have anything similar to one. Your income funds your lifestyle. A reduction in your income will require an adjustment to your retirement goals. That means you need to be clear on priorities.

Here are some of the questions to address: How much income will you need in retirement? How will taxes and inflation affect that income stream? If your spouse dies, will the income be less? How much Social Security income will you lose? How much pension income will you lose? How much of that will you need to replace or make up? Do you have a plan to replace those dollars?

You should differentiate your discretionary and nondiscretionary expenses. Your nondiscretionary money is what pays your mortgage and utilities and health insurance and puts food on the table and gas in the car. Those are essential "needs," and that income should typically come from secure, guaranteed, consistent sources. Meanwhile, other sources can pay for your "wants"—perhaps a special vacation, or a golf-club membership. You can accept more risk with how you invest that money, if you wish.

YOU DESERVE PEACE OF MIND

In this book, I want to make it clear that you can set up a plan that will give you security and peace of mind for the rest of your life. That plan will take into consideration your individual needs as well as your goals and desires for yourself, your family, and for posterity.

In these pages, you will find a wealth of advice on a wide range of topics of concern to retirees. You will learn what to look for in a good advisor, for example, and you will see the importance of teamwork. You will get tips on taxes and fees and on how to afford long-term illness care. I will help you understand issues of inflation and other threats to wealth and well-being.

These are issues that weigh heavily on retirees' minds. I want to reassure you that you can move forward with confidence and freedom from debilitating fears. Yes, it is likely that you will see money falling through the cracks, but now you will be able to see those cracks and take steps to repair your portfolio. You can do that with the guidance of a qualified advisor.

In my twenty-plus years of financial planning, I have seen daily the issues that people face as they prepare for retirement. Often, nobody has pointed out to them the critical matters that will intimately influence the quality of the years ahead. They haven't heard this from their advisor, or broker, or CPA, or attorney. None has provided the retirement advice they truly need. As a result, many retirees remain unaware of how they could direct more money to what matters most to them.

Many retirees—and those on the cusp of retirement—learned a harsh lesson in 2008. They need not have suffered that way if only the proper advice had reached their ears. I want to do my part to remedy that situation so that millions of retirees can remain securely on the path to prosperity.

CHAPTER 1

What Went Wrong?

Mark and Sue Dimarco did all the right things. They bought a home, put their kids through college, saved for retirement, and worked with a broker to establish a "conservative" investment portfolio so they could have an ideal retirement. Their goal was to retire a little early, but a major portion of their investments were wiped out in the market correction of 2001–2002. They were told to "hang in there," so they worked for an additional four and a half years until their portfolio value returned.

In 2007 Mark and Sue again reached their financial goal and were again ready to retire. They wanted to know where to put their money so it would earn a reasonable rate of return, provide steady retirement income, and—unlike the last time—be safe from market losses. This time the plan is working, despite a major market correction from 2007 to 2009.

What did they do differently?

· · · · · · · ·

Jake and Anna Reinhardt's story is much the same. They both worked and saved for retirement, forgoing many indulgences during their working years because they planned to travel and enjoy life after retiring. But their savings and investments were annihilated by the 2007–2009 market correction, and they couldn't afford to retire. Rather than traveling and enjoying what they expected to be doing in their retirement years, they had to go back to work, postponing their dreams.

After meeting with their advisor, they expected to work five to 10 more years before they could "re-retire," a plan that was shattered when Jake suffered a heart attack in 2012 and was forced to stop working. With their income sharply reduced and their health-care costs through the roof, Jake and Anna's retirement lifestyle is a far cry from what they had envisioned.

Does their story sound familiar?

· · · · · · · ·

Beverly Marler, a widow, told her advisor that she didn't want to lose her money and was comfortable with a conservative return. She was advised to invest her $1.5 million into a "conservative" portfolio that he set up for her. This was her entire financial security.

As the market corrected from 2007 to 2009, her broker told her to "hang in there, the market always comes back." In the meantime, Beverly relied on income from her portfolio and had to take required minimum distributions from her IRA accounts, so the nest egg continued to shrink. Her broker then advised her to reduce her income withdrawals so she wouldn't outlive her money.

Even though she did "all the right things," Beverly is living on less income, and her financial security has seriously eroded. She can't afford to travel as much, so she stays home while her friends head off to many of the places she had long dreamed of visiting.

Doesn't she deserve better?

· · · · · · · ·

When **Jim and Marsha Richards** retired, they thought they were well prepared to continue their comfortable lifestyle. After all, Jim, a former executive, had put away a significant amount of savings for retirement. Plus, they had been working with not one but two brokers who advised them how to invest. Then, when the market took a downturn, the Richards lost a sizable chunk of their savings, and they were hit with a significant tax liability because of how their investments were structured.

What went wrong?

· · · · · · · ·

Harvey and Karen Moore were living comfortably off their Social Security income and Harvey's pension benefits. But when Harvey died, his pension "died with him." This, combined with the reduction in Social Security income after Harvey's death, reduced Karen's monthly income by nearly 65 percent, even though her expenses remained virtually unchanged. Her lifestyle is dramatically different now.

Could this have been avoided?

. . . .

Lynette Lowry had a good state pension, so she was able to leave $500,000 in her retirement account to her daughter. However, the bequest put the daughter and the daughter's husband in the highest tax bracket and pushed their own earnings into that bracket as well. And nobody advised them that they had to remove the money from the retirement account within a set period, so there was a late penalty fee of 50 percent. The total approximate tax liability of that account was pretty much the entire value of the account.

Their tax problem had nothing to do with the market's performance. It resulted from failing to make sure those funds were positioned properly. It resulted from the all-too-common stance of "I don't need the money, so I'll just leave it where it is; I'm afraid of change." The mother thought she was doing a good thing for her daughter. Instead, she did it all for the IRS.

. . . .

These are real scenarios, real people. I used different names to protect their identities, but I'm sharing their stories because chances are that you or someone you know is in a similar situation. Maybe you're scared that something like this might happen to you. That's probably why you're reading this book.

There is an epidemic of financial uncertainty among retirees today. For example:

- Over 86 percent of Americans don't feel well-informed about generating retirement income, investing their nest eggs, or managing their risks in retirement.

- Less than 40 percent plan for more than 20 years of retirement, despite today's extended life expectancies.

- Just 25 percent think they're saving enough for retirement.

- Very few retirees factor in how they might cover the escalating costs of health care and long-term care and generally rising prices due to inflation. They don't consider what they will do if they outlive their savings.

When did retirement get so complicated? And who has been there to help you figure it all out? When all those 401(k) plans replaced pensions, did anyone help you determine whether you were contributing enough? Did anyone help you decide how to manage and allocate your funds, or how to convert your retirement accounts to secure income in retirement? Probably not.

You had to learn how to drive and take a test before you were given your driver's license, right? At summer camp, someone made sure you could swim proficiently before you were allowed in the deep end. But was any training required for managing your financial life? For most people, financial education has been nonexistent.

Most of the people in the previous stories did do "all the right things"—that is, all the right things for accumulating assets during their working years. When they approached retirement, what went wrong was that they failed to shift the emphasis to the preservation of those accumulated savings. At that point, preventing the erosion of principal and making plans for distribution should become the priorities.

Many people make a huge mistake when moving from the accumulation phase into the preservation stage. After years of investing in risk-type funds, it can be very difficult to taper off the risk and make the transition to a preservation mindset. Failing to do so has produced a very real problem facing most Americans today: the fear of running out of money before they die.

The Wall Street lie is that even though the people in our stories lost money, they shouldn't feel bad because everyone else did too. But in truth, everyone didn't lose money. Why? In many cases it was because they did the following:

- They went through a "look-forward" discovery process.

- They learned the right questions to ask and problems to solve.

- They planned properly, and they followed that plan.

Not only did these people not lose money, but they actually increased their financial security during a time of insecurity for most. How was that possible? That's what this book is all about.

CHAPTER 2

Your New World

Retirement is a time of redefinition, particularly in these days when so many of the rules and expectations seem to have been revised. Some may imagine long days of lounging at poolside or on a porch, but that's far from the reality. Many retirees are busier than ever and might come to wonder how they ever had time to hold down a full-time job. They often do find a job, perhaps part-time, that they enjoy doing. Others look forward to traveling and spending time with family and grandchildren.

The goal is achieving the financial independence to pursue the active and healthy lifestyle that they have long envisioned. They have dreamed about all the things they will do, and now their time has arrived. Seldom do retirees struggle to find ways to fill all that time. It should be an exciting new freedom to do what they want, when they want, how they want. Financial security means different things to different people, but those who continue to work should be doing so because they enjoy what they do, not because they must do it to survive.

INCOME NEEDS DO NOT DECREASE

With the active lifestyle of retirement—the hobbies, the interests, the travel—the need for income is not decreasing. It's either staying the same or increasing. That runs counter to the advice that people often hear: that they won't need as much income in retirement. A lot of times, particularly early in retirement, people are pursuing the pent-up desires they have harbored for years, such as traveling, and they have seven days a week to spend their money, rather than just on weekends.

People also are often advised that they will be in a lower tax bracket when they retire. That was the premise that led to the proliferation of 401(k) retirement accounts, which defer taxes until the money is withdrawn. The reasoning goes like this: You will save on taxes when you start spending your money in retirement. That's because you will be in a lower bracket. The trouble is this: You probably won't. Not only will you likely have as much income as ever in retirement, but the tax rate is likely to rise. We will be taking a closer look at this in Chapter 6.

And retirees face other tax pressures. Among them is this: If they pay off the house, there is no more mortgage deduction. When the kids have moved out, you lose those deductions for dependents. Retirees simply do not have the write-offs that they used to have. Often they have not considered these things, and nobody has pointed them out.

THE SOCIAL SECURITY MISNOMER

The demographics of the United States are changing dramatically as droves of baby boomers begin to head into retirement. We are going to have more people on Social Security, with far fewer people working and paying into the system, but those people on Social Security are going to receive it for significantly more years than their parents did. We are on an unsustainable path.

Often couples will show me their Social Security statements, and together they are scheduled to receive about $4,000 to $5,000 per month when they begin receiving their benefits. How could that possibly be sustainable for the 78 million boomers being added to the system? The truth of the matter is no secret: It's right there on your Social Security statements, page one, upper right paragraph.

About Social Security's future …

Social Security is a compact between generations. Since 1935, America has kept the promise of security for its workers and their families. Now, however, the Social Security system is facing serious financial problems, and action is needed soon to make sure the system will be sound when today's younger workers are ready for retirement. Without changes, in 2033 the Social Security Trust Fund will be able to pay only about 75 cents for each dollar of scheduled benefits. We need to resolve these issues soon to make sure Social Security continues to provide a foundation of protection for future generations.

This cannot continue. The foundation upon which Social Security is based has shifted and weakened. People live far longer now than they did in the '30s, so there are not enough workers to support them. Yet the Social Security check has become such an entrenched part of our expectations for retirement that it's a political mess for anybody who forecasts trouble and attempts to do something about the pending problem.

We do know, however, that Social Security somehow will have to change from the way it looks now. In the past, Congress has increased taxes on benefits and deferred them until later years, and that pattern is likely to continue as the government grapples with how to sustain the system.

Changes are inevitable. It would be a mistake for a retiree to just factor in Social Security to retirement income and presume nothing will eat away at that source. If you are 80, you indeed may not see much happen to your benefits. But if you are 55, you can expect some rules to change. It's important to understand that you may need to become more dependent on your own savings and less dependent on government programs such as Social Security.

AN EXCITING TIME, A FRIGHTENING TIME

Retirement is a time of joyful anticipation—and often, doubts and misgivings. It's not unusual to encounter troubled feelings as you launch into retirement. For one thing, so much of people's self-identity has been tied up in career and work. That's something that's hard for them to talk about, but sometimes a sadness sets in as the retiree misses the bustle and responsibility and authority experienced in the workplace. Retirees can lose part of their sense of self.

Nonetheless, most people are ready to be done with work, and they're excited about moving on to the next phase of life. For a few years, they attend to projects that they have long wanted to do, whether it's a home improvement or a self-improvement. Eventually those projects are done. What does life look like from there?

Everyone is different in that situation. Many retirees want to travel, enjoy more of that free time, pursue those hobbies, maybe start a business, do more charity work, or spend more time with the grandchildren. Whatever your inclinations, it is important to seriously consider what you want to do with the rest of your life. An advisor needs to know your goals in order to offer any meaningful help with an income plan.

If I were to say in one word what many retirees are seeking, I would say "significance." They are concerned about the mark that they will leave on the world. Did they make a difference? What did they want their life to stand for? I see a lot of that as people get older and they have more freedom. Their focus shifts to making a difference.

THE CHANGING NATURE OF YOUR WORRIES

Earlier in your life, you concerned yourself with starting a family, buying a house, raising children, saving for college. You probably saw your debt load increasing. You strove to advance in your career, keep those raises coming, and pursue a more ambitious lifestyle.

In retirement, you have launched your children into the world. You may still have a mortgage on your house—in fact, for tax reasons, it's good if you do—but many of those concerns you had when you were younger are now gone. An increasing number of boomers find themselves dealing with taking care of children and elderly parents at the same time, but eventually those issues fade away. You have gone through your peak earning years and settled many of your responsibilities, and you are looking forward to the freedom to do what you want.

One adjustment that retirees must face—and a particularly troubling one—is the sudden cessation of the paycheck that came so dependably all those years. They have to make their own paycheck now. That can be quite an unsettling realization. They generally don't have a pension to fall back on anymore. Do they have enough to be able to afford retirement? Are their assets positioned properly to create that income? Will a change in the market or economy affect their financial security and retirement, influence their lifestyle, and alter the course of their lives?

Such concerns are common among retirees. Based on what I hear from clients, the most frequently expressed worries involve the prospect of running out of money, or of becoming ill or incapacitated. Let's take a look at several of those concerns. Later chapters will deal with many of them in more detail:

- **Health-care concerns.** A major concern for retirees is the cost of health care and long-term care and how rapidly those expenses have been rising. People often are uncertain about how much they need to set aside. Some haven't considered what can happen. It can be fatal to your retirement if you get sick and you haven't planned for it properly. But you need not despair that your life savings could be for naught. There are a lot of things you can do, as we will discuss in Chapter 9. In my observation, it's the middle classes to the above-middle classes that are most concerned about health-care costs. The lower-income people, with fewer assets, are most concerned about outliving their money. Interestingly, people of above-average net worth—say, $5 million to $10 million—also are most concerned about outliving their money. Though their lifestyle certainly is different, they still wonder if they can afford to retire, and they worry whether their assets are positioned properly.

- **Long-term care.** The chance that you'll have some long-term illness continues to increase. It seems that every new study makes that patently clear. Retirees worry about that, but many of them don't like long-term-care insurance because either it's too expensive, or they can't qualify, or they feel that "if I don't need it, I lose all that money."

Many retirees simply have not been informed about the myriad of solutions that could overcome those issues.

- **Stock market losses.** Retirees also worry that the stock market is going to smack them down, and often they do not understand that there is an alternative to staying in the stock market. Studies show that people are much happier once they have income streams that they know will be coming in regardless of what happens in the economy. Wall Street and the media have long told them to just persevere and they will be all right. But that leaves retirees sweating over how a market correction affects them now. That can directly influence their retirement lifestyle. It's not only a matter of how the equities perform; it's also the time required to manage them. Do you want to spend a few hours every day staring at the computer, weighing your winners and losers, or do you want to travel and see the grandchildren and not have those worries?

- **Taxes.** Retirees often are concerned that they are paying too much in taxes. The more that goes to taxes, the less that can stay in the investment portfolio to grow and compound. When you pay less to the IRS, you can build greater long-term financial security and be better buttressed against inflation. Nonetheless, we often find that when people hit retirement, particularly in the first few years, the amount of taxes they pay goes up a little more each year just because of incorrect planning.

- **Liquidity.** A common concern among retirees is whether they will have access to their money when they need it. As a result, they end up leaving too much money sitting in the bank and getting low rates of return. "What if something happens?" they reason. "I can't risk not being able to get at my money." Often that plays into other fundamental fears, such as a health crisis or long-term illness. Determining how much liquidity you need is certainly smart, but it doesn't mean that money should just be parked in the bank. Money in the bank is lazy money because it is earning next to nothing. You should only keep enough in the bank for true emergencies.

- **Inflation.** The one common denominator that retirees all seem to misunderstand is the impact of inflation on their nest egg. It eats away at it steadily. People think that they have enough money to retire because they're looking at today's dollars. They do not consider what inflation will do to the value of those dollars over the course of the twenty, thirty, or forty years that they or their spouse are likely to live.

- **Interest rates.** "Where can I put my money so it's safe," they ask, "and still earn a fair rate of return. Is that even possible?" With their money at risk in the stock market, retirees tend to wonder whether they are spending too much or too little. They just don't know what they can spend. They make comments such as, "Well, Wall Street says I can spend 4 percent each year, and I hope they're right, because if they're wrong I won't make it." They're afraid.

One of two things happens. They spend significantly less than they could, and perhaps in their later years they regret that they did not take that trip or buy that special gift or give more to charity. On the other hand, perhaps they do lose that money in the market, or due to the erosion of inflation. They just don't know how things will turn out. That's the value of an income plan: you can calculate how much money you need for essential expenses and position your assets properly to generate it. Then you will know how much you have in addition to that for nonessential expenses.

- **Estate planning.** A retirement goal for many is to plan for posterity: how much can they leave to their children and grandchildren and other heirs, and how much can go to charity. Retirees need to consider whether their assets are positioned properly in that regard. If they have a trust, is it set up efficiently? Are there any bear traps in that trust? Often people don't understand that there are certain assets that are better suited to leave behind. Some are good for use while you are living, and some are good for distribution of your wealth after you have died. There are some assets that are great for passing to children and grandchildren. You can leave so much more behind if you use the right types of vehicles in the right types of situations.

TAMING THE UNCERTAINTIES

With careful planning, many of those uncertainties can be eliminated. You can know whether you have enough money to last the rest of your life and whether you can spend more. How sad to learn someday that you were incredibly frugal throughout your retirement years just because you were afraid, when you truly could have done a whole lot more. Then again, poor planning can also lead you to a false sense of confidence. All those variables add up to a good reason to go to a professional and develop a thorough understanding of your financial situation.

Remember: The strategies that you used during your accumulation years are no longer appropriate. In fact, they can be quite counterproductive at retirement age. Your investments cannot tolerate as much risk at this stage. However, you still must stay ahead of inflation, which you probably didn't really consider much during all those years when you got raises that kept pace with it. Now, if you don't factor in inflation, your nest egg can begin to evaporate. Things will simply cost more, diminishing the value of your savings. Those who retired in 1990 have to spend $1.77 today to buy what cost a dollar back then. Or let's say you have $500,000 now, and inflation continues at an average pace of 3.5 percent for 25 years. That same amount in 25 years will have the purchasing power of only $212,000 in today's dollars. You will need well over a million in 25 years to equal what $500,000 is worth today.

YOU ARE NOT ALONE

These are universal concerns for retirees, and I have heard them expressed many times. These same issues have kept many a retiree awake at night. I help people sort through these concerns so that they can have the most productive retirement possible. I'm not a stockbroker, and I'm not trying to peddle anything. I want retirees to have peace of mind so that they can enjoy their lives without fear of financial trouble. When they put their heads to the pillow, they won't stay awake wondering about the "what if's."

I have three children. Two are new drivers: our daughter, who is 18, and our older son, who is 16. When you are teaching young people to drive, you sit in that passenger seat in full knowledge of things that they have yet to understand. You prepare them to head out on their own. They don't know all the questions, they don't see all the dangers, but you know about them—and all too well. You have seen what can happen. It's similar when helping people prepare for retirement. You are helping them steer clear of danger. You are giving them peace of mind so that they can enjoy retirement, free of worries. They know that all the important questions have been addressed.

Those worries are certainly justified. So many things can wreck a retirement plan: illness, a crash in the stock market, emergencies, divorce, or the death of your spouse. However, they all can be anticipated. The likelihood of any of those can be discussed in advance so that they don't catch you off guard. Come what may, you can have a fulfilling retirement.

CHAPTER 3

Ever Onward

On the road to retirement, people typically begin to think about what they have always wanted to do and what they will leave behind when they are gone. How will they be remembered?

Until you know your goals and priorities, you can't create an effective retirement plan. You can't plan until you know what you want to do. There's generally no point in setting out on a trip and consulting a map if you don't have any destination in mind. You need to know where you are going. An effective retirement plan must be tailored to your specific needs and goals.

Boomers define retirement in many ways. I work with a couple who want to retire in several years, buy an RV, travel the country for a while, and then come back and work part time. Another couple has retired and is still working—but in jobs they enjoy, free of stress. And yet another couple I know has fulfilled their dream of starting a business.

Everybody's retirement is different, but the common goal should be to reach financial security, and since many retirees nowadays are in excellent health and easily can anticipate three decades in retirement, they need to plan for many years to come. With financial security, the hours that used to be consumed by work and career will now be spent on hobbies or activities with friends old and new.

Usually retirees have been able to save a good amount of money during their peak earning years, and they will need it to fund the lifestyle that they have dreamed about. Someone may have told them they would likely be able to live on a lot less during retirement. Someone told them wrong. An active life of travel and friends and fun is expensive.

RISK OF SPENDING TOO MUCH—OR TOO LITTLE

If you don't have a plan with specific goals, if you don't know where your resources will take you and how long they will last you, you may live in fear unnecessarily, embarrassed by your frugality. You may spend less than you truly can afford. Years later, in failing health, you may look back with regrets over unfulfilled dreams.

Or perhaps your lack of perspective about your financial situation will lead you to take too many risks that deplete your savings and compromise your financial security. Or you may simply spend too much. Later in life, you have to cut back drastically. I have seen the sad consequences: You can end up feeling alienated from friends who no longer invite you on outings because you might not be able to afford the cost.

How pathetic to be telling yourself some day, "If only I had planned better, this wouldn't have happened." Or how pathetic to have missed out on life's joys because you simply were scared. Both extremes are sad and so very avoidable. It's not that people plan to fail, but they do fail to plan.

IDENTIFYING YOUR GOALS AND DREAMS

To bring greater clarity to the course of your retirement, you need to take stock of your life goals and organize them by priority. Just what are your dreams and goals? You should write them down as a tangible part of your financial plan. Ask yourself specific questions and write down what comes to mind: What and who are important to you? Whom do you wish to help? What do you want to learn? Where do you want to go? What makes you feel happy? Fulfilled? What have you always wished you had time to do? Do you have a "bucket list"?

Take a peek into your future as you imagine it will be: Do you see yourself traveling? Daily rounds of golf? Indulging in a hobby? Spending time with grandchildren? Do you plan to work part time or perhaps volunteer for charities? Do you intend to help other family members financially?

YOUR GOALS MUST BE REALISTIC

You need to identify what, in your personal situation, are your discretionary and nondiscretionary expenses. How much do you want to spend to attain your personal goals, and how much must you spend to survive? As we will discuss in

Chapter 8, your nondiscretionary expenses should be funded through guaranteed income sources. That way you need not worry about running out of money for your essentials.

It's important to get a handle on the withdrawal rate that you will need to fund the lifestyle you desire. Consider what will happen if your investments don't go the way you expect. Your lifestyle could change dramatically. You may find yourself unable to keep pace with your golf buddies. If maintaining those relationships is of high importance to you, does your retirement plan allow you to maintain them under any circumstances? In other words, are you truly being realistic about the kind of lifestyle that your portfolio can provide?

Many people simply are not clear about how much they can or cannot take from their portfolio. They don't know what they can afford. No one has taught them this information, so they base decisions on their experiences. But those experiences can be misleading. For decades, the stock market seemed to go ever upward, as did real estate. But the "normal" has changed. Those investors have since faced significant struggles. It's important to recognize what can happen if you base your lifestyle on the support of fluctuating economic cycles. Like all friends, they can let you down.

Baby boomers tend to perceive the market's performance based on how it did when they began their investment life—in other words, phenomenally. It's only recently, since the turn of the millennium, that their eyes have been opened. It's human nature to extrapolate our experiences into expectations. Retirees thus are led to withdraw from their accounts even as they sink, fully expecting that the market will make it all better. After all, that's what it did in the past. But that's not necessarily what it will do in the future—and once they start those withdrawals, the situation worsens dramatically.

Meanwhile, inflation affects retirees disproportionately, as the rapidly rising cost of medical care illustrates. If high inflation, such as we saw in the Carter administration, rears when you are retiring, you can be devastated. Inflation may have averaged only a few percent a year over the generations, but you're not dealing with an average. You're dealing with you. You're dealing with what you are facing now in the real world, and that's why you need to be realistic about your dreams. You have to plan for the worst even as you are hoping for the best.

MATCHING DREAMS WITH RESOURCES

It helps to identify the date when you wish to achieve such financial security, and then to identify what might get in the way of that, such as a market correction, significant inflation, an increase in taxes, or health issues. Your dreams, in other words, must match your resources. If you don't have a handle on that, you will face troubles, including that feeling of social isolation when you can't keep pace with your friends.

PACK THE RIGHT LUGGAGE FOR RETIREMENT

The lesson is clear: It's important to organize your life. You have to organize your goals, your dreams, and your priorities so that you know where you are going. A good retirement advisor can help you get there. And a good planner also can help you organize your documents so that your financial life flows as smoothly as possible and so that your heirs don't face a nightmare upon your passing.

Suppose you are going on vacation: If you are headed to the ski slopes, you pack your bags differently than you do if you are headed to the islands. Retirees who want to worry less about financial issues should pack their bags differently than someone who still has twenty or thirty years to go before reaching retirement.

If you go to the beach and you bring only ski jackets to wear, you are probably not going to have a lot of fun on that trip. Nor do you want your bathing suit for the snow. You will not be properly outfitted for the conditions. You need to have the right luggage, and you need to pack appropriately for the prevailing climate. In other words, you need to thoroughly analyze your assets and your liabilities and your expectations. The goal is to make sure that your financial affairs are organized in a way to support what you want your retirement to look like.

ORGANIZING YOUR DOCUMENTS

In our first meeting with clients, we request that they bring a variety of documents with them so that we can be of help.

Then we ask them to complete a confidential questionnaire. We want to know who they are, and what their family situation looks like. What are their goals and concerns, and what is the state of their finances? What type of investments do they have? Do they own any real estate? What are their tax issues? Do they have life insurance? Who are their heirs? We ask that type of question because we need to know up front whom we are dealing with.

We also take a close look at their tax return. We want to look at the financial statements. How are their assets allocated currently, according to their goals? We look at their Social Security statements or their pension statements to help them make the appropriate decisions at the appropriate times to make sure they have enough income now and later.

We want to look at their estate planning documents: Do they have a will or a trust, and what assets are in the trust? Is it set up properly? We examine their life insurance and other coverages. If they have rental property, do they have the right liability insurance? Do they have the right health insurance, and are they making the right changes if they are moving toward Medicare? Do they have any kind of long-term-care protection?

We want to see the big picture. We want to listen to goals, dreams, desires, fears, concerns. And then we want to help our clients put a plan in place so they can make the right decisions as they move forward.

Where should you keep your important papers? A lot of people store things digitally, and some people put them in safe deposit boxes. I find that it makes the most sense to have copies of your important documents scanned into the system of your retirement planner, who specializes in your particular needs. Your planner will have them there for safekeeping.

That's the value of a retirement planner: to make sure everything comes together efficiently. We were recently working with a couple when the husband passed away after three years of suffering from dementia in long-term care. When the widow came to our office, we were able to produce everything needed: the various documents, insurance papers, funeral plans. We already had a plan in place to reach out to the life insurer and get the benefit to her right away. We reached out to the children and got them up to speed. We reached out to the Social Security officials and to the credit card companies.

Because everything is scanned in electronically, we have easy and secure access. That makes it convenient for the children and the surviving spouse. And when that spouse dies, we again have everything ready for the heirs: an accounting of the assets, the legal documents, beneficiary designation forms, and other necessary papers. We explain what needs to be set up and how to handle matters properly. And we provide essential tax advice on how to distribute assets appropriately, preserving income now to meet needs later.

Typically, your financial advisor will organize all of your documents into a binder. It contains everything necessary to manage your estate while you are alive, and to settle and distribute it after you pass away. Most people retain the originals of those documents in a safe at home, making sure that the appropriate people—successors, trustees, beneficiaries—have a key or the combination. If you choose to keep things in a safe deposit box at the bank, be certain that one or more of your adult children are signers on that box.

Above all, however, work with a retirement advisor who not only will have those documents scanned and organized and ready when needed, but who also will have your plan of action ready as well. Organizing your files helps you to organize your life priorities and to clarify your direction in retirement, and that makes it all the more likely you will reach those goals, and more.

CHAPTER 4

A Matter of Trust

The pilot taxies down the runway and waits to be cleared for takeoff. He knows the routine. He lives by the clock—boarding and takeoff and arrival times. Before the jet leaves the ground, he is well aware of the destination and conditions. He doesn't just fly aimlessly a few hours before checking in with air traffic control and asking, "So, hey, where am I supposed to be landing today? Are we on track?"

That pilot is constantly making tweaks and corrections to speed and altitude and direction, based on conditions encountered— wind direction and turbulence, for example—so that you land safely on time at the desired destination. The slightest miscalculation could put you off course by hundreds of miles and many hours.

What you want from your pilot is a safe takeoff and landing, and you would appreciate a comfortable ride in between. You got on board to reach a destination, not to experience stunt thrills. You want a competent pilot whom you can trust to do his utmost to take care of you.

The pilot's job is not to predict the storm. The pilot's job is to plan for it. A retirement planner's job is similar. If your advisor comes back and says, "Look, the market had a correction, but hang in there; it will come back," that is not a plan. There's no preparation there. That is riding the stunt plane.

What people typically want in a retirement is the smooth ride. They want a comfortable retirement without worries. They don't want to hear, in the wake of a market correction, that they need to take less income or they will run out. They don't want to hear that they should sell their home, downsize, and invest the difference because they have lost too much in the stock market, or have to reduce their investment income. That strategy depends on predicting the market, and that's not our job as retirement planners. Our job is not to predict the next market correction; rather, it is to make sure you are prepared for it so that when it does happen, you don't lose your financial security.

You certainly don't want to hear the pilot of an airplane announce, "We have encountered some turbulence, but we're probably going to make it." That just isn't good enough. You have to know. But that is the essence of what a broker is telling you when he or she says to just hang in there after a correction and everything will turn out all right, probably.

BAD ADVICE ALL AROUND

Many people in my industry who present themselves as financial advisors are putting retirees at huge risk. They persist in pursuing strategies of growth that are appropriate for young investors but generally unwise for older investors. Most advisors wear rose-colored glasses when it comes to the market, believing it will always go back up, but retirees cannot accept that level of risk.

Stockbrokers typically operate in the world of accumulation, and retirees have advanced beyond that world. It's true that making money involves some risk, but it's important to identify the money that is appropriate to subject to risk. Just as a gambler shouldn't risk the mortgage money, likewise investors must not risk money that they need for essential expenses. When you have years to recover, you can take more risk, but in retirement you must be particularly careful to identify the money that must be kept safe. A stockbroker, who has a Wall Street mindset, is not likely to lead you in the right direction.

Nor will you likely get much good advice from the media. Understand that the media hype certain products. The majority of *Money* magazine's advertisement income, for example, comes from mutual funds. Open up the magazine and you will see mostly mutual fund ads. Nothing wrong with that, but keep in mind that what you read will have a bias toward promoting mutual funds. The media look to sell the news. Their job is not to teach you how to invest safely and securely. They focus instead on the peaks and valleys of the market, and that reinforces the risk mentality.

Beware the advice you get at cocktail parties or from the crowd around the water cooler. Everyone wants to offer you a tip on what's hot and what's not, but that's a far cry from real planning. Likewise, a friend or acquaintance who has done well in the market might offer you advice, but what makes sense for one person could be disaster for another. Your friend may be able to accept risk that you cannot.

For example, a woman who was referred to me was receiving an inheritance of about $1 million. She never had much money before, and wanted to use the inheritance for a retirement income. Her brother, a multimillionaire, told her to just invest that money in the stock market and manage it. "He spends most of his day every day managing his portfolio," she told me, "and he's admitted that he's lost significant money when the market has gone down, but he doesn't need that money." You might find someone whom you respect who has done well, but what works for that person certainly may not be the best advice for you.

The Internet is another major source of questionable advice. It is information overload, and it is impossible to learn everything. While it's important to do research, you don't have to learn about and understand every type of financial product that's out there. It's important to understand what's happening in the economy, of course, but you should focus on what you can change. You can't change tax rates, but you can change the amount of tax that you pay. You can't control the stock market, but you can control your risk and manage your rates of return. You can't control inflation, but if you are aware of it, you can strive to maintain your buying power.

As you are bombarded with information and advice, you need to keep a simple perspective: Your own unique situation is what matters, and you need to learn the questions to ask and which problems need to be solved to assure yourself a comfortable retirement.

HOW IS YOUR ADVISOR PAID?

Many advisors are commission-based, meaning they make money by selling you a product. As a result, your goals and their goals may be at odds. If the market goes up, you're certainly happy and they are happy too. If the market goes down, you're not happy, but they're still happy. Their financial incentive is not connected to your financial incentive. Their goal is to just sell you an investment and receive a commission.

The standard for advisors who work on commission is to offer you suitable investments. For example, such an advisor might sell you a mutual fund that does all right even though its fees are above average and the rate of return is nothing to brag about. It's still suitable for you, though it may not be better than most others. From the advisor's perspective, however, it may come with a commission that's better than most, and the advisor finds that quite suitable, indeed.

The commission model may be appropriate for investors with the financial sophistication to make their own choices and manage their portfolios themselves. Perhaps they feel secure with their income from a pension and Social Security and other sources and feel competent to take on risk. They're just looking for someone to help them make a particular trade. They don't need someone to help them do the research; they can determine on their own what makes sense. When dealing with advisors who earn commissions, it is the buyer's responsibility to determine what is appropriate. For savvy and experienced investors, how the advisor is paid may be less of a concern.

On the other hand, many investors will want a financial advisor who has a fiduciary responsibility to determine your overall plan and what investment or investments are in your best interest. The advisor helps you to determine what makes the most sense for you, looks at the options and investments available, and determines which are most appropriate, the ones with the lowest fees and reasonable turnover and rate of return. He or she will recommend investments that are the best fit for your situation.

Advisors with fiduciary responsibility typically don't receive a commission. They generally charge a fee for their services, and that fee is usually a percentage of assets. That percentage usually decreases for larger portfolios, and the fee also depends on how much you want the advisor to do for you.

A fee-based advisor is more in line with your goals. As a fiduciary, the advisor has to do what is in your best interest at all times. But the money incentive is there as well: When your portfolio goes up, you both are happy, of course, but if it goes down, both of you are unhappy. The advisor makes less in fees if your assets are diminished.

Attorneys and CPAs have fiduciary responsibility to work in your best interest. In the field of financial planning, a registered investment advisor has fiduciary responsibility. If you are getting advice from a fiduciary, the money you pay may be tax-deductible. The IRS considers it to be money spent for professional, competent, knowledgeable advice. On the other hand, it considers a commission to be a sales charge, and it is not deductible.

You would consider a doctor to be a quack if he greeted you at the door with a smile, handed you a prescription without examining you, and said, "Here, take this, it's the best thing since sliced bread." You expect that a doctor will run tests and carefully consider your symptoms. However, in the financial industry, clients often let advisors tell them, "Here, invest in this, it's the best thing since sliced bread." There's no examination of your particular needs.

WHAT YOU NEED IN AN ADVISOR

A good advisor should tailor a plan that is appropriate for you and that considers your unique needs and goals. In order to do that, you need to establish a strong relationship. You need thorough communication and a good rapport.

Such an advisor will do far more than lead you to investments based on what they have done in the past. He or she will not merely sell you a product touting a great return and a five-star Morningstar rating. Advisors who do that are mainly helping themselves, not necessarily you. That's just buying a product. A plan helps you to identify your goals and look at what you are trying to accomplish from the standpoints of income planning, tax planning, and risk management.

There are five prime areas of concern for retirees: longevity, risk management, inflation, health, and taxes. A good advisor will consider all those aspects and put in place a plan, with regular reviews to make sure you are staying on track and to identify any changes that are needed. Different economic cycles and tax environments will require different strategies.

In looking for a qualified advisor, ask your other professionals for referrals. You will want a registered investment advisor with fiduciary responsibility. And when you identify a prospect, find out how his or her clients did during previous market corrections. Did they lose money? You want to check the advisor's background and look for any complaints. How many years of experience does the advisor have, and is that experience in retirement planning specifically? These are questions that you shouldn't be hesitant to bring right up. A good advisor will be happy to answer them.

YOU NEED A TEAM AND COACH

It's important to make sure that your professionals are working together. One thing that we recommend is to meet at least once a year with your financial advisor and your CPA in the same room to review your plan and to identify changes that should be made.

Teamwork is essential. You need somebody who really understands your situation, who doesn't just come out and recommend a few investments to buy and hold and just be patient. Together, you need to identify goals and how to reach them, and monitor how you are doing. Your primary financial advisor should reach out to your other professionals, such as the attorney who makes sure you have documents set up correctly, and the CPA who is looking at your finances from a tax standpoint.

For a professional baseball player to get into the major leagues, he must hit the ball consistently. He will have coaches to help him develop that talent. Once he is in the big leagues, at the top of his game, he still will have coaches working to help him stay there. Likewise, golfers often hire a coach who can provide the knowledge and tips to improve their game. Even the pros in their golfing prime continue to use coaches. They never feel as if they cannot improve. You too need a coach who can help you identify and maintain the best practices with your finances.

YOU MAINTAIN THE CONTROL

In working with an advisor, you are in effect delegating responsibility. You are at the top of your game as you approach retirement because you played it so well all those years of your career. But your game isn't necessarily the financial game. Your game was whatever it was that brought you prosperity. You've succeeded in your niche.

Any good CEO delegates and surrounds himself or herself with people who know how to do things better, such as the chief operational officer or chief financial officer. That's good leadership. You have to have someone on your side who specializes in exactly what it is you need to do. The same responsible sense of leadership that brought you success in your career will also foster your success in retirement.

You are not losing control. You actually have more control because you have identified your goals and the risks that you are facing. You can see how your plan will help you reach your goals and overcome those challenges, and you can gauge whether you are on track. The typical retiree finds that a good plan provides a sense of being in charge of one's destiny.

SEALING UP THE CRACKS

It's very likely that your team will discover that you have money falling through the cracks. This is usually due to taking a fragmented approach to the handling of taxes, investments, insurance, income and estate planning. For example, many people separately use a CPA to file tax returns; a banker to purchase CDs; a broker to buy stocks, bonds, or mutual funds; an insurance agent to purchase life insurance; and an attorney to draft a will or living trust.

Each of these professionals meets a need, but no one is integrating the various elements into an overall strategy. Money is lost without you or your various advisors even realizing it. You could be losing money to unnecessary income taxes, to low rates of return, or to those investments that keep bleeding as you wait for them to get "back to even."

Many retirement advisors work closely with the kind of team you need: the estate attorney, insurance agent, CPA. If you can find a practice that uses this type of business model, it's a good bet that you'll receive advice that minimizes the amount of money that's falling through the cracks.

It's time to take control of your money. Taking control doesn't necessarily mean doing everything by yourself. Rather, the best way to create financial security in this uncertain world is to take a coordinated approach to your tax, investment, income and estate planning. And the best way to do that is to work closely with a team of like-minded professionals.

Even if you prefer to keep working with your current broker, attorney or CPA, you need to know what questions to ask and what problems need to be solved. That requires them to operate as a team, each with specific areas of expertise. It's their job to stay on top of the rapid pace of change in their industries, and they're also experienced in addressing the needs of retirees and their families in all kinds of situations. For example:

- *Healthy, vigorous retirees* who want to make sure they remain financially able to maintain their active lifestyle. Poor planning can strip retirees of the lifestyle they once had. You should be having fun and thriving in your retirement, not scaling back or living with financial insecurity.

- *Retirees with health problems* or who are facing an uncertain diagnosis. If you're facing health trouble, you need to focus your resources and energy on getting better, not worrying about how to make ends meet financially. Working with people experienced in guiding others through similar situations can spell the difference between despair and peace of mind.

- *The loved ones of retirees,* particularly those with power of attorney, who want to make sure they understand how to protect the assets of their spouse, life partner, or parents. Again, working with a team of financial and legal professionals avoids confusion and instills confidence.

HOW TO FIND THE RIGHT PROFESSIONALS

Here are a few tips for finding the right guides for your retirement journey:

If It Sounds Too Good to Be True, It Probably Is

It's a common and scary trend today to hear retirees who have made poor decisions based on "buying into great opportunities." If a financial salesperson tells you about a 9 percent CD when you know the bank down the road is paying 1.25 percent on CDs, you should be seeing a red flag—a giant, waving red flag. When you hear about something that sounds good and you want to believe it, ask this simple question: "So, what are the strings attached?" If the person peddling the product says "no strings," then you need to turn and run. There are a lot of great financial products with attractive features. But even the great opportunities out there come with "rules" (aka "strings attached"). You need to know what they are and whether they are acceptable to you and in line with your planning goals. Always trust your own good judgment and common sense.

Is the Advisor a Fiduciary?

Again, let me emphasize that financial advisors who are considered fiduciaries are required by law to put their clients' best interests first, before their own. Working with a fiduciary means working with a "registered investment advisor" (RIA) as opposed to a "broker-dealer representative." It's their fiduciary duty to provide the very best solutions they can for their clients. Most financial professionals, including many who sell products on commission, are not fiduciaries and are only held to the "suitability" standard. That doesn't necessarily mean what they are selling is the best option available, and it certainly doesn't mean it's the best option for you. Someone who immediately urges you to buy a financial product before reviewing your situation is not the advisor you want. Look instead for someone who takes the time to listen and walk you through a process, rather than simply selling you a product.

Beware of Online "Resources"

You may be tempted to use the Internet as your "advisor," but information online should be viewed with a very skeptical eye. Today it is not uncommon for retirees to jump online to do research. The critical question is whether you are getting information from a credible source. Information overload is another problem. If you enter the keyword "revocable trust" on Google, you'll come up with millions of articles, websites, and "resources" to look at. Before you could possibly look at all those online entries, you'd be dead and your family would be burdened by the costs and delays of probate! Yes, you need to do research, but research the right topic: "finding good help." Focus your due diligence on finding the right planning team to assist you.

Is the Advisor Accomplished?

There's nothing worse than being sold a bad idea. Slick talk can be persuasive, but it may prove financially disastrous. When seeking professional advice, we recommend that you assess just how accomplished your prospects really are.

For example, do they answer your questions, and ask you the right ones? Many advisors may be well versed in growth strategies for the accumulation stage of financial life, but sorely lacking when it comes to the preservation and distribution of assets. Likewise, they might be good at developing retirement income strategies but not at identifying ways to reduce taxation. Look for someone who specializes in working with retirees and takes a coordinated approach to tax, investments, income, and estate planning.

Is the advisor well known and well regarded in the community and industry? Advisors build a good name for themselves when they really know their stuff. Media outlets, for example, are looking for experts because they want their viewers, readers, or listeners to get credible and accurate information. True professionals are those who believe in their expertise strongly enough to go on record with their knowledge and insights.

Do they invest in their professional knowledge? This question is a great way to gauge the prospective advisor's commitment to staying current on new laws, tax-code changes, and cutting-edge ideas to help preserve and grow your wealth. If you have a large IRA, for example, you might be swayed by the fact that the advisor has specialized training in IRA planning.

Be Smart and Trust Your Feelings

Much is revealed when you meet face to face. See how you feel. We believe that every person who walks through our office doors should be treated like a member of our own family, and other practices do business in the same way. Sure, credentials are important, but so is your gut feeling. Do you trust these people to help you design and follow your financial retirement strategy? If the answer is no, keep looking for the right fit. Find a team that fully understands your concerns, challenges, and priorities. Credentials are important, but so is your gut feeling. Do you trust these people to help you design and follow your dream?

WATCH OUT FOR YOUR BLIND SPOT

No matter how vigilant a driver might be in checking mirrors, there may be a "blind spot" where it is difficult to see another motorist approaching. And in situations like that, having a friend along for the ride can be a life saver. You need someone with a different perspective from your own, someone who can see things you can't, someone who can help you make a little adjustment to avoid an unfortunate consequence.

I have met hundreds of people who are in a similar position financially. They are cruising along, minding all the laws, doing everything they know they should be doing. They think everything is perfectly fine, but creeping up in their blind spot are some significant financial issues. With the volatile market, the economy in turmoil, and the financial uncertainty we all continue to face, so much is at stake. You simply can't afford a wreck at this point, when you should be enjoying retirement.

That's why it's a good move to have an expert with a different perspective review your current financial approach. There's a chance you may arrive at your retirement destination just fine. But with so many variables to consider, and so much that you may not be able to see from where you're sitting, isn't it worth making sure?

CHAPTER 5

More Complex than Ever

Here's the simple truth: Millions of retirees are crowding onto a broken three-legged stool, the floor underneath it has given way, and the Chinese government holds the mortgage on the house. Makes sense? After you read this chapter, it will.

With apologies to the Beatles, allow me to change a line to "Eleanor Rigby" as befitting the baby-boom generation: "Ah, look at all the retired people." As you see in the chart on the following page, the number of US retirees is rising and expected to reach unprecedented levels in the years to come. That is the result of millions of boomers reaching retirement age. In the next twenty years, an average of more than 10,000 people will be retiring every day. And they will stay retired longer: The average life expectancy is 78. Half of today's 65-year-old men are expected to live to age 85, and half of today's 65-year-old women are expected to live to 88 (see chart on the next page).

No wonder so many people are worried that their money won't last as long as they will. Consider this: For the first time in history

Population 65 Years and Older by Size and Percent of Total Population: 1900 to 2010

(For more information on confidentiality protection, nonsampling error, and definitions, see *www.census.gov /prod/cen2010/doc/sf1.pdf*)

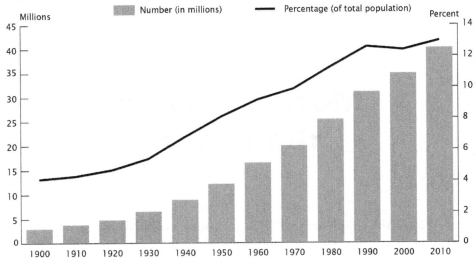

Sources: U.S. Census Bureau, decennial census of population, 1900 to 2000; *2010 Census Summary File 1.*

Life Expectancy in the US, 1929 and 2007

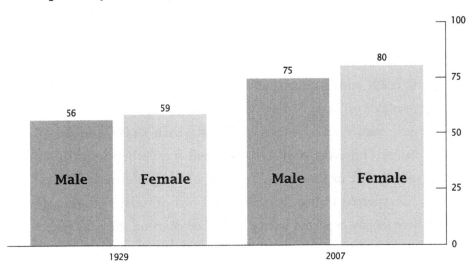

Figures obtained from www.census.gov: http://www.census.gov/statab/hist/HS-16.pdf and http://www.census.gov/compendia/statab/2012/tables/12s0104.pdf

there are now two full generations of retirees: baby boomers and their parents. This may be great for family reunions, but it's wreaking havoc on traditional ways of planning financially for retirement. Let's investigate further.

THE BROKEN STOOL

In the old days, planning for retirement was simple. You'd just rely on the "three-legged stool." We talked about that rickety old stool in the Introduction. Let's take a closer look at what has happened to it and what retirees face in today's uncertain environment.

These are the three legs that propped up that stool: an employee pension, Social Security income, and personal savings and investments. Between then and now, however, each leg has been altered, strained, broken, or chipped away to the point that the stool can't be relied on for secure and reliable support.

DEFINED PENSIONS, MOSTLY A MEMORY

Back in the day, the defined benefit pension plan was a virtually guaranteed source of steady income in retirement. The amount of pension benefits received depended on how long a person worked at a company (or institution or government entity) and at what age he or she stopped working there. From these figures, employers calculated precisely how much the person would receive in monthly or annual pension benefits after retirement.

Pensions were steady and predictable—that is, unless the employer went out of business or the pension was otherwise underfunded, an increasing reality for many state and federal workers, both civilian and military. Although most employers began phasing out defined benefit pensions in the 1980s, they are still responsible for paying out the benefits owed to the now mostly retired employees who worked there when the pension plan was in place. Where the money will come from to make good on this promise remains to be seen in the cases of federal retirement programs with an unfunded liability of $5.7 trillion.

Only about 15 percent of today's workers are covered by defined benefit pension plans, which have been all but replaced in the private sector by 401(k) savings programs. However, if you are among those who currently receive, or will receive, pension benefits, it is important to consider what will happen to those benefits when you die. In some cases benefits will continue to be paid to your spouse or other designee. In most cases, however, pension benefits are either reduced by half or stop altogether when the owner of the pension dies. And that, of course, can have a huge impact on the surviving spouse's retirement income and standard of living.

401(K)S—BE CAREFUL WHAT YOU ASK FOR!

Basically, phasing out pension plans in favor of 401(k)s shifted the investment risk from employers to employees, who are responsible for designating automatic deposits from their earnings into the accounts. The employer also may contribute to the 401(k), matching the employee's contribution to a certain percentage or dollar amount. Usually there are several investment categories to choose from—stocks, bonds, money markets, mutual funds, and so on—and you allocate the percentage of your overall contribution that you want to go into each category. The employee's financial security is dependent not only on the allocation choices he or she makes, but also on the performance of the underlying investments chosen.

Prior to the late 1990s, most people assumed that most or all of the 401(k) investment options were relatively low risk—that is, until markets around the world took a sharp dive, popping many a nest-egg bubble. Such downturns have caused about 27 percent of workers aged 45 and above to delay their retirement.

HIDDEN FEES IN MUTUAL FUNDS

Mutual funds, a fixture in 401(k) plans, include a variety of fees within them. One study found that most people are unaware of the extent of those fees. They don't realize the huge impact that their 401(k) plans' fees can have in the long run. The 401(k) fees can be 2 percent to 3 percent annually, or even higher. Reducing these fees by just 0.5 percent a year over thirty years will increase income in retirement by 10 percent. Reducing fees by 1 percent will increase income in retirement by a whopping 20 percent!

In addition to those fees are the trading costs involved in managing the funds. The trading cost will depend on the turnover—in other words, the percentage of the assets within the fund that are turned over or replaced in a year's time. That could certainly increase the trading costs inside that mutual fund.

Many times people will hold several mutual funds in the belief that they are diversifying, but when you look at the investments inside the mutual funds, you discover a lot of overlap. The diversification is an illusion. The higher fees that result, however, are very real.

These internal fees are often considered to be hidden fees because under current law they do not need to be made available to the individual investor. These are not the external, disclosed fees; they are buried inside the mutual fund, and investors are not made aware of how much the fees total. It's because of those fees that about 85 percent of mutual funds do not outperform benchmarks such as the Dow Jones Industrial Average or the Standard & Poor's 500.

Even if you were inclined to read the prospectus, you will not find all the fees. One example of a fee within mutual funds is the 12b-1 fee. It is basically a marketing fee. The mutual fund can use that money to advertise and market its fund, buying advertisements in, let's say, *Money* magazine. The fund is charging you a fee to advertise itself to other people. You also may want to ask yourself what happens when the fund is full and not accepting new investors? Will that 12b-1 fee be eliminated? All too often, the answer is no.

To reduce the amount they are paying in fees, some people will move their money to low-cost, index-based mutual funds and ETFs. That will most certainly reduce the fees. You have addressed one of the concerns, but you still have risk that needs to be managed.

MUTUAL FUND ABUSE

The original concept of the mutual fund was to allow small investors to diversify their portfolios to reduce risk. The theory is that paying percentage fees for that service is fair and acceptable. However, mutual funds have been abused by our industry and are used in far too many cases or situations where they shouldn't be used.

Investing in mutual funds works for someone who has perhaps up to $250,000 in financial assets, and that's at the very high end. Once you are getting near that much in assets or more, it's best to look at other types of investment options. You typically will mature and grow beyond what mutual funds can offer you in terms of managing risk, rate of return, tax situations, and fees. They will tend to pale in comparison to what other investments can do for you. Still, mutual funds are appropriate for a small investor who is looking to have a better diversification than just a small basket of stocks.

In choosing mutual funds, most people look for one that did the best for the last three years. History shows that the mutual funds that were at the top the last three years are typically not at the top after that, so that is not an appropriate way to pick mutual funds. Unfortunately, that's how most mutual funds are sold: "Look at this one, it's a five-star fund and what a return! So put your money here!" The salesman gets a fine commission, and you get stuck with a dog that underperforms the market.

Buy-and-hold strategies do not work for mutual funds because a portfolio manager continues to buy and sell. You may decide to hold on, but if someone else in that mutual fund decides to cash out and cut his losses, the manager must sell investments so that can happen. When the fund sells at a loss, you suffer those losses because you still are in it. You are not really buying and holding; other investors in the fund are forcing the sale.

SOCIAL SECURITY, WOBBLY AT BEST

Let's take a closer look at that second wobbly leg of the retirement stool. Social Security was created in 1935 as part of President Franklin D. Roosevelt's New Deal. It was intended to limit the poverty rate among senior citizens, which exceeded 50 percent after the stock market crash of 1929 and subsequent bank failures destroyed the value of many Americans' nest eggs.

Twenty years later, in 1955, there were approximately nine workers "paying in" to the system for each one receiving Social Security income. Today that ratio has dropped to 3:1, and it's expected to slip to 2:1 over the next twenty years. The economics of the system simply cannot be sustained over the long term at current benefit and tax rates. Beginning in 2010, the program started to pay out more in benefits and expenses than it collects in taxes each year.

According to the US government, Social Security has an unfunded liability of $6.5 trillion. However, if the program's shortfall was calculated in the way that a corporation would assess the financial obligations of its retirement program, that unfunded liability would jump to $24.1 trillion. Because of this shaky funding, Congress is likely to reduce and/or delay Social Security benefits as well as increase taxes on those benefits in the years to come. Realistic retirees view Social Security as merely a supplement to more stable income sources.

PERSONAL SAVINGS UNDER ASSAULT

In many cases today, the 401(k) or similar plan is the retiree's only savings. What has happened is that the first and third legs of the traditional planning stool—pensions and personal savings—have been combined into one leg, and you don't need to be a physicist to figure out how that is likely to affect the stool's stability.

Even among those who do have savings set aside in addition to their 401(k) or pension, most do not really know how to leverage their money into reliable, accessible income during retirement. Moreover, they often base the amount of retirement income they will need on current numbers, without considering inflation, higher health-care costs, increased taxes, and global market conditions.

Each of those plays a major role in defining one's true standard of living and how far those personal savings will stretch. A recent study by Americans for Secure Retirement found that 86 percent of Americans are worried about maintaining a comfortable standard of living in retirement. That's up from 73 percent in 2010.

Yet most baby boomers fail to factor inflation correctly into their savings and income strategies, despite the fact that it can wipe out the prospects of a comfortable retirement. If you are retiring now with an income stream of $75,000, in twenty-five years at the typical inflation rate you will need about $160,000 a year for the same purchasing power. In other words: Much will be demanded of your personal savings.

Among those inflationary pressures is the cost of health care, which has continued to rise at an alarming rate. Health-care expenses have been shooting up at double to triple the general inflation rate for a decade. Between 2000 and 2009, medical and prescription medication costs as well as health insurance premiums and deductibles increased by almost 150 percent. In 2011, health-care costs rose 5.75 percent per capita during a period of otherwise low inflation.

Unfortunately, no one predicts that this climb will slow in the foreseeable future. The effect on retirees can be particularly harsh. One study projects medical costs in retirement for the average, healthy 65-year-old male to be roughly $369,000, not including insurance premiums. And this doesn't even take long-term care into consideration, an expensive reality that approximately two out of three people over 65 will need.

Taxes are another formidable threat to your personal savings. Tax rates today are somewhat lower than they have been in past years. However, when you consider the unfunded liabilities of Medicare and Social Security, along with the staggering size of the national debt, taxes are destined to rise. When that happens, what will be the impact on your investments and on your retirement income? How can you make sure that your savings stay in your pocket to produce income for you, not for the IRS? The next chapter will deal with those questions and more.

IS WALL STREET THE ANSWER?

Faced with such assaults on your personal savings, you may be thinking your best option is to sink your savings into the stock market, but the market, particularly in these times of global uncertainty, is a scary place for many retirees. In the last decade, both the Dow and the S&P 500 have averaged a return of just about 3 percent a year. Many people have referred to this as the "lost decade." Will the stock markets of the world be safe or dangerous to retirees and those planning for retirement in years to come?

Wall Street has historically said you should be able to withdraw 4 percent a year from your diversified portfolio of stocks and bonds and never run out of money. This rule might have made sense when investors were earning 6 percent or more on their investments. But if you had followed this advice over the last ten years, the value of your portfolio would very likely be worth approximately 43 percent less than it was a decade ago. For those in this situation, the choices are as follows:

- Continue taking the same income and hope you die before you run out of money;

- Withdraw less income and marginalize your lifestyle;

- Stop income withdrawals altogether and go back to work while waiting for your funds to grow back to where they were before.

Obviously, none of those options are appealing. But it's even more complicated than that. The stock market as we have known it in past eras is a totally different animal today. Real-time, 24/7 trading on a global basis brings the ups and downs experienced by economies around the world to the fore for US investors, and more often than not, the results are less than optimal.

The world is awash in dollars that the US Treasury has pumped out to deal with the financial market mess and its own deficit spending. In 2011 the US government borrowed 40 cents of every dollar it spent, and its biggest creditor is the Chinese government.

TAKE CONTROL OF YOUR FINANCIAL FUTURE

Don't lose hope. Even in today's uncertain environment, there are ways to prepare for and enjoy a secure, comfortable retirement.

When you're not feeling well, typically you relate your symptoms to your doctor, who may run some tests, and, based on the results, make a recommendation, perhaps for a medication, or exercises, or a change in diet. The doctor might recommend that you see a specialist. That's the kind of relationship you should have with a financial advisor. Just as in the practice of medicine, there's a logical, systematic process to identify your financial "symptoms," obstacles, and challenges, and to arrive at solutions for your unique situation.

This is what I call a "look-forward" approach. To get the full picture of your financial situation, you need to take an in-depth look at your taxes, your risk exposure in contrast to your risk comfort level, and your income needs in retirement. No recommendation can be appropriate unless you and your advisor are clear about these matters.

Without preparation, the many financial challenges that retirees face add up to a significant threat to their security. In the chapters ahead, we will take a closer look at how to deal with some of the greatest of those challenges. But first I'd like to point something out that might give you a new perspective: We usually discover, when we review these matters with clients, that they are letting at least $3,000 to $5,000 fall through the cracks each year. Over ten years, that's $30,000. Those with above-average income or higher net worth are often losing considerably more: $10,000, $20,000, even $50,000 a year.

Let's say you needlessly lost $5,000 last year. What if that's been going on for the last decade? Can you afford to lose $50,000? Certainly not when you're depending on your savings to provide steady income during retirement. Think about what you could do with that amount of money: travel, help put a grandchild through college, or remodel the kitchen. Or you could invest it safely for income in the future.

There are many good ways, of course, that you could spend or invest the money. The point is that it could be there for you and your loved ones. You just need to redirect it. You need to take control of your financial future. If you are losing money, just when would you like to find out? Now? Or never?

CHAPTER 6

Tax Reduction Strategies

Picture this: It's April and all your friends and family members are complaining about their taxes going up again. Do you dare tell them that yours are the lowest you can remember? Go ahead. Then tell them how you did it.

In this chapter, we will look at several tax-reduction strategies that are guaranteed to save you money. This is not a primer on how to lie, cheat, or steal from the IRS. To the contrary, these are simply ways to avoid common mistakes that result in paying more taxes than you owe.

TAX PREPARATION VERSUS TAX PLANNING

Start by asking yourself this: Is the person who prepares your taxes a preparer or a planner? Most CPAs are tax preparers. You provide them with your 1099s, W2s, and so on, and they prepare your tax return by putting the right numbers in the right boxes. Then, depending on what you have already paid in tax during the year, you either receive a refund or pay additional tax. The next year you repeat the process.

A CPA or financial advisor who is also a tax planner, however, will call you later in the year and invite you back in for an appointment to review your tax return and financial statements in order to do a better job the next time around.

Your tax return is a map to help you save on taxes. There are most likely several things you can do to pay less moving forward. Rather than just filing a copy of your tax return away, you can review it and identify strategies. As you and your advisor conduct a review, line item by line item, you likely will encounter those errors that are draining your assets.

The most common mistake that people make is paying tax on income that they earned but that they didn't spend. To explain this clearly to clients, I use a "bucket" system that illustrates how money should be handled for tax efficiency.

YOUR "NOW," "LATER," AND "NEVER" BUCKETS

The typical retiree has one bucket into which all income flows and, in turn, spills out onto their tax return. For example, let's say one of your investments suffers a loss, and yet it still paid out a distribution during the tax year. That must appear as income on your tax return. Even if you're growing an asset to give away to your heirs or a favorite charity or financial advisor, it still may be flowing onto your tax return as income.

Some of the most common items in the bucket are earned income, rental income, pension and Social Security income, IRA distributions, interest, dividends, and capital gains. More than likely you're paying taxes on this income whether or not you're spending it. Whether or not you need that income to live on now, in the near future, or never, you're paying tax on it yearly. It doesn't make sense.

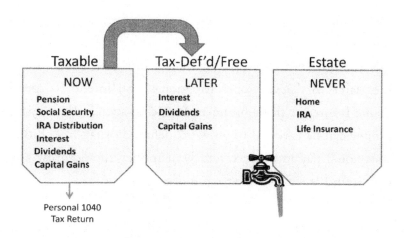

Consider this: Say you want a glass of water. You go to the faucet and turn on the water. When the glass is full, you turn off the faucet. So why don't you just leave it running all the time? Then you could put a glass under the faucet whenever you wanted some water without having to turn it on and off. You don't do that, of course, because it would be a complete waste of water.

Yet the same thing is probably happening on your tax return every year. All of your income is running full blast onto your tax return whether you spent it or not. The result is that you pay more in income tax than you need to pay.

There are some common types of income sources that you might not be spending: taxable interest income, for example. If you didn't spend that income in a given year, you still have to pay tax on it. Ditto for dividends and capital gains.

Once you have identified where you have been paying tax on money that you don't need now for income, you can move that money from your one big bucket into two smaller ones, the "later" or "never" ones for money you intend to spend in the future, or that you never intend to spend. There, your money can be invested to grow tax deferred or tax-free. Either way, you'll pay less in tax, and your money should grow and compound at a faster rate than it does now.

Tax-free investments include Roth IRAs, municipal bonds, and cash value life insurance, to name a few. Tax-deferred investments include retirement plans such as traditional IRAs and 401(k)s, annuities, health savings accounts (HSAs), and so on. Depending on how they are deployed, those can have distinct advantages over taxable investments, which include mutual funds, certificates of deposit, and stocks that generate a dividend.

Bottom line: When using this process, your first bucket, the "now" bucket, should only contain income sources that you are spending now, in the short term. Consider repositioning other income sources in your second and third buckets, where the money will grow, either tax-deferred or tax-free, for later use or for passing on to your heirs.

Assets in your "later" bucket can be invested with a longer term philosophy, using growth strategies that can perhaps generate higher rates of return to accommodate your future needs. Think of this bucket as having a control valve or spigot on the side so you can turn on an income stream or simply withdraw funds whenever additional income is needed, and then turn it back off when not needed. That way, you control how much tax will be paid.

During your preretirement years, the assets in your "later" bucket can be left to grow, then transition to "now" income during retirement. This bucket is also available if you experience a loss of income—say, if Social Security or pension income is reduced after the death of a spouse. You also might want to reach into your "later" bucket for one-time expenses, such as taking a trip, updating a home, or purchasing a car.

Your third bucket, or your "never" money, is for estate planning. These are assets you intend to pass on after your death to family members, charities, or both. Some common examples would be your home, IRA account, life insurance benefit, and so on.

Are there taxes associated with these assets? Yes. There could be capital gains tax, income tax and, if your estate is large enough, there may be state and federal estate taxes. Even if you're "skipping a generation" to avoid taxation on the assets, there may be a generation-skipping transfer tax. Nonetheless, if you can identify the assets that you intend to pass on, you also can identify the taxes that are associated with them and take steps to reduce or eliminate those taxes.

TAX SAVINGS MEAN GREATER ASSETS

Here is the simple truth about why all this matters: If your money is growing without tax, it compounds at a faster rate, which increases your income and helps you safeguard against inflation.

If you can avoid paying tax on money that you earned but did not spend, you can keep your after-tax income the same simply by reducing the amount going to Uncle Sam. That means you will not have to withdraw as much from your savings and investments, an obvious advantage, or if you prefer, paying less in tax will allow you to increase your after-tax income and cash flow and enhance your standard of living.

Is your advisor talking to you about these things? Does he or she ask you to bring in your tax return to see how you can do a better job of reducing taxes in the year, and years, to come? A good financial advisor can help you position your assets in the right "buckets" to ensure that a) you're not paying unnecessary taxes year after year, and b) you have a long-term income strategy for a successful, comfortable retirement.

By identifying what each of your assets is designed for—short-term use, generating income, growth for future income or emergencies, or passing on to heirs or charity—you can make much more informed and advantageous decisions about how to position your money. You might not even be aware of some of the taxes that can sap the strength of your portfolio, and this simple process will help you regain control of your finances.

ELIMINATING "PHANTOM INCOME" TAXATION

Experience shows that about 85 percent of people are affected by "phantom income" taxation, yet very few people understand what it is. It's possible to owe taxes on dividends or distributions that you receive from investments, even when they're losing money. How? Here are three of the most common scenarios:

Stocks and mutual funds. Let's say you have a mutual fund that showed an overall loss for the year, but the fund manager sold some of the stocks within it at a profit. You would receive a capital gain distribution for that portion of the investment even if the fund value declined. On paper you lost money for the year, yet you still paid taxes on it (or some of it, anyway). This is what's known as phantom income taxation.

If, for example, you received a $10,000 distribution from a $300,000 stock portfolio, you probably would pay at least 15 percent to 20 percent income tax on it, or approximately $2,000, and the added income could trigger a tax on your Social Security benefit. That would be the case even if the investment dropped 10 percent that year, or $30,000 in value. Not only did you lose the $30,000, but you also lost $2,000 to taxes.

Bonds. People typically buy bonds because they've been told they're a safe investment, which is generally true as long as interest rates stay low. When interest rates rise, which they inevitably will, the value of many types of bonds can dramatically decrease. Phantom income can come into play with the taxable earnings from bonds. You receive the earnings and pay tax on them even though the bonds dropped in value during the year.

Real estate. In today's depressed real estate market, it's very easy for phantom income to emerge on the real estate front. Say, for example, you receive $10,000 in rental income for the year (which is taxable) even though the value of the property dropped $30,000 for the year. That's another example of a painful truth: You can find yourself paying taxes even when you have realized a loss. The tax man has a way of adding insult to injury.

As we review our clients' finances, phantom income taxation is often one of the first cracks that we discover money falling through. And since many investors have much of their assets devoted to mutual funds, let's take a closer look at the mechanics of how the phantom tax affects them.

When considering a specific mutual fund, you look at its rating, fees, investments, risk, and rate of return. But another thing to consider is the amount of selling and buying within the fund. If a fund's turnover is 50 percent, that means it sold and repurchased half of the portfolio in a year's time. A turnover of 100 percent means it replaced the entire portfolio.

The turnovers can be quite extensive. I recently met with a client who had a mutual fund with a 732 percent turnover. That means that the entire portfolio was turned over seven times. You can imagine the extent of the trading fees involved in that. One must wonder why a fund would consider it a good strategy to turn over half of everything it has on the table every month. If these are quality investments, why must they be bought and sold so rapidly? That invariably will lead to excessive trading costs and hurt the rate of return.

All of that buying and selling within a mutual fund can generate phantom income, even when the fund experiences a loss overall. And along with that phantom income, you can get phantom income taxation. At the end of the year, when you get your mutual fund statement, you will see that you have lost, let's say, $20,000. You are frustrated enough by that, but then you receive a 1099 that says you have a capital gain of $10,000. "Wait a second," you exclaim, "how is that possible?" It's because every time the fund sells an investment, any gain must be reported to you in the form of a 1099. At the end of the year, though you've lost money in investments, you can actually have a capital gain.

Your portfolio is actually less than you started with, but you still have to pay tax on that phantom gain. It comes down to this: You're paying tax on money you lost. This particular tax is one that has directly contributed to the weakening of that three-legged stool of retirement planning. Many retirees have much of their life's savings in mutual funds within their 401(k) plans. With the disappearance of pensions, those 401(k) plans were touted as their replacement, but we must beware of their pitfalls.

SOCIAL SECURITY TAXATION

Many people are needlessly paying taxes on their Social Security income. Depending on your circumstances, up to 85 percent of your benefit can be considered income subject to tax. That may be enough to force more tax on your other income sources by pushing you into a higher tax bracket. For many people, this can be eliminated.

Example: The combined income from Bob's CD interest and required distributions from his IRA were enough to force him to pay tax on his Social Security income. This resulted in a tax liability of $5,000 for the year.

By repositioning his CDs into tax-deferred or tax-free investment(s), he would no longer receive a 1099 from the bank, so he wouldn't have to report the earnings on his tax return. His IRA distributions alone may no longer be enough to require tax on any of his Social Security income. The net result is that his tax liability for the year would have gone from $5,000 to only $500. This represents an annual tax savings of $4,500. Over ten years, that's $45,000.

TAX-ADVANTAGED PAYOUT STRATEGIES

Tax-advantaged payout (TAP) strategies allow you to take money from your tax-deferred "later" bucket and have about 90 percent of this income be considered tax-free. If 90 percent is tax-free income, that means you're paying significantly less tax.

Example:

$10,000 of income at 25 percent tax bracket = $2,500 in tax.

If 90 percent of that $10,000 is tax-free, that means only 10 percent (or $1,000) is taxable. That's a tax savings of $2,250. In other words, on $10,000 of income, your net income is $9,750 instead of $7,500, an increase of $2,250 in your pocket.

Using a tax-advantaged payout strategy, you may be able to generate significantly more after-tax income, starting with the same amount of money. Not only could this help you pay less in tax on your other income sources, but it also may move you into a lower tax bracket, even if tax rates increase in the future. In addition, dependent on your unique situation, implementing this strategy properly could reduce or possibly even eliminate tax on your Social Security income.

TAP strategies can help two types of retirees:

- Those who lost too much in the market or didn't have enough saved to retire comfortably and are looking for ways to increase their after-tax income;

- Those who are financially secure but want to utilize strategies that provide income using the least amount of financial resources possible, allowing for a greater percentage of their investments to be used for other purposes.

Make sure you and your advisors understand tax-advantaged payout strategies and how to apply them. The question to ask is, "How can I take my income in retirement in the most tax-advantageous manner?"

PROPER TITLING OF RETIREMENT ACCOUNT BENEFICIARY FORMS

You should also review whether your retirement account beneficiary forms are filled out correctly. This isn't going to help you personally; it's more for your spouse and your heirs.

Example: Tom's parents died, leaving him as the beneficiary of their assets. An attorney and a CPA together settled the estate and transferred the assets to Tom, who received a check. Later he learned that some of this inheritance came from an IRA, meaning that it was 100 percent taxable. This put Tom in a higher tax bracket. Not only did he have to pay more in tax because of the IRA funds, he also had to pay more in tax on his earned income. Once the funds were removed from the deceased's IRA account, it was too late and nothing could be done to fix it. It was all taxable and created a tax nightmare for Tom.

The key is to identify things like this before it's too late. Had the beneficiary designation forms been set up correctly, the IRA funds that Tom received could have continued to grow, tax-deferred, for multiple generations. There wouldn't have been any additional tax on his own income. He could have controlled how much was taxable and decided when he wanted to pay the tax, rather than all at once.

Take a $500,000 IRA as an example. When this asset passes to the heir, or heirs, at death, it's all taxable income. If the estate is large enough, there could also be state and/or federal estate taxes. The "tax spiral" could be anywhere from 65 percent to as much as 80 percent, meaning that a $500,000 IRA would be worth about $175,000 at death. Plus, the heirs will most likely have to pay additional income tax on their personal income.

There's a simple fix for this, known as a MGIRA (multigenerational IRA). You don't need anything special to set it up; you do so simply in the way you complete your beneficiary designation forms. It's still your money; you don't lose control. It simply allows the heirs to inherit the IRA balance and pay no tax up front; the account continues to grow, tax-deferred except for required minimum distributions over one or more generations. That means that the $500,000 IRA, instead of only being worth $175,000 at death, could easily pay out more than $2 million over time, due to the longer period of deferral.

BENEFITS OF FULL OR PARTIAL ROTH CONVERSION

Named for its chief legislative sponsor, Senator William Roth of Delaware, the Roth IRA is in many ways preferable to traditional retirement accounts. The main difference between a

Roth IRA and most other tax-advantaged retirement plans is this: Instead of granting a tax break on money when it is placed into the plan, the Roth IRA grants a tax break when it is withdrawn.

Let's compare the traditional retirement account to the Roth IRA. The traditional IRA is 100 percent taxable. Required minimum distributions (RMDs) begin at age 70½ and continue for the rest of your life. You therefore are putting money into an account where the IRS tells you when to take it out, how much to take out, and how much tax to pay. Based on the federal debt and the direction that tax rates are heading, I would call that a "tax hostile" asset.

The funds in a Roth IRA are 100 percent tax-free, including the principal you invest and all earnings inside the account. There are no RMDs during the account holder's lifetime. Simply put, you have to pay tax on any funds deposited into this account, but they grow tax-free, and under current tax law you are never required to withdraw this money during your lifetime. But, even if you do withdraw these funds, the income tax liability will still be zero.

Your financial advisor can help you determine whether a Roth conversion would make sense for you—that is, whether you should convert your traditional retirement plan into a Roth by paying the taxes up front so that you will not be required to pay them when you withdraw money.

ADDING UP TO SIGNIFICANT SAVINGS

A thorough review of your tax situation can find ways for you to save significantly, but you must ask yourself whether your advisors are catching these kinds of details on your tax returns. Even when people have a financial advisor, CPA, and an attorney review their returns, it is still possible that none of them will see any of the opportunities for them to pay less tax.

Do you get the feeling that maybe, just possibly, you might have some money falling through the cracks of your tax returns? If you could identify where that's happening and redirect the money to what's most important to you, would it help you build greater financial security? Might it help you to not outlive your money, be better prepared for inflation, leave a legacy to your heirs?

Think about it: Do you want the IRS to be your biggest beneficiary, at the expense of your family or the institutions and causes that mean the most to you?

CHAPTER 7

Reducing Risk and Increasing Returns

Once you are at the point of financial security, it's as if you have a winning lottery ticket. You wouldn't drive down the freeway waving it out the window. You would guard it carefully.

You need to preserve your savings by managing risk while also doing your best to get a good return because inflation is one of the greatest risks of all. You only have one chance to do this right. If that money flies out the window, your retirement is going to be compromised, or you're going to have to go to work, or maybe you will risk running out of money. We all know stories of people who were in that situation.

You must not wait until your last day of work before starting your retirement planning. It should happen prior to retirement. Are you on track? Are your funds allocated appropriately to reach your specific goals at a particular time?

Picture that coworker at the water cooler back in 2007. In his mind he's probably adding up how much is in his 401(k), how much more he'll be adding, his rate of return, how much his employer will add, and what he'll have when he retires in five years. He's probably already picking out his vacation home. And along comes the correction, and he's derailed. His retirement isn't what he envisioned. Perhaps he just had to work a few extra years, or, worst case, he's laid off. The fact of the matter is he only has one person to blame and that's himself. In 2007, when he had five years to go to retirement, he should have been sitting down and putting a plan together. He should have been addressing what he had to do to move from accumulation to preservation appropriately.

SOME MAJOR RISKS

Let's recap a few of the major risks that can threaten your retirement portfolio:

Sequence of Return Risk

An asset might average a rate of return of 10 percent over time, but that doesn't mean that is how much your portfolio will grow. It's an average of good years and not-so-good ones, and what really matters is their sequence—in other words, whether the good years come early or later. Do you experience losses early on as you're saving when you're young, or do you experience those percentage losses when your portfolio is larger?

Sequence of return risk can wreck your portfolio in retirement if you make regular withdrawals from an account that rises and falls with the market. True, you need a return that will stay ahead of inflation, but at this stage of life you have limited time to recover from a market correction. You will also need income for your retirement years, and you may believe that tapping your account for 4 percent each year couldn't hurt. After all, you tell yourself, over all those years your portfolio averaged an 8 percent return. But remember this: Over all those years, you weren't withdrawing; you were adding. Good years came and bad ones came, and the order didn't matter because this was for the long run. Now, in retirement, the long run has become the short run, and if a bear market hits you early, your nest egg will suffer. On paper, that long-term 8 percent average is still true. In reality, your portfolio could wither. The market indeed does well over time, but you must not count on it doing well in the early years of your retirement.

Inflation Risk

In this economy of low interest rates, inflation is certainly a risk as people park their money in low-yielding environments. CDs are an example. Typically their net return is a negative, because inflation can be growing faster than their actual return. Though your portfolio may show slight increases, every year it has less purchasing power.

Withdrawing from a Sinking Account

The amount of any losses also is important. If you lose 30 percent, you need a gain of 43 percent to break even. If you lose 50 percent, you need a gain of 100 percent—and that's just to get back to where you were.

Many boomers, during the drop from the end of 2007 to the beginning of 2009, saw their portfolio crash. Many of them were still able to work and add to their retirement accounts. Maybe their employer was still adding, and they didn't need to take any money from the account, so within a few years they were back to where they were before.

However, think of those who were retired during that period of time. As retirees, they typically were not adding to their portfolios, and in fact they probably also were withdrawing money for income. Those people's savings are still off by about 30 to 40 percent. How the market affects a portfolio and the amount of time it takes to get back to the breakeven point is very different for the person who is still working than it is for a retiree who is withdrawing income.

REQUIRED RETURN TO REGAIN YOUR PRINCIPAL

% LOST	% GAIN NEEDED
20%	25%
30%	42.86%
40%	66.67%
50%	100%

TAKING RISK OFF THE TABLE

As you move closer to retirement, it's important to take some of that risk off the table. You must identify the income that you need, and you must understand the difference between needs and wants. You should draw on safe, guaranteed sources to pay for what you absolutely must spend. Only if you don't need the money should you put it at risk.

If you do it that way, any losses you experience will be less likely to harm you because you will not be withdrawing from the account. You thereby eliminate sequence of return risk. You can afford the time it takes for your account to get back to breakeven.

Taking risk off the table does not mean switching to risk investments that are supposedly more conservative. It means making the appropriate changes to truly eliminating some risk.

THREE FINANCIAL WORLDS

Earlier we discussed how people should move from the accumulation phase of life during their younger, working years, and then to the preservation phase during retirement and eventually to the distribution of their assets. Similarly, there are three typical financial stages in which we learn how money works. First we learn about the world of bank savings, then about the investment world of Wall Street, and then about investments with insurance companies.

The first stage of people's financial experience is typically bank savings. Maybe as a child you were saving up for something, a bicycle, perhaps, and your parents helped you open a savings account to which you could add money. Or you may have made some income on a paper route, or received some birthday money from Grandma, and that money too went into the savings account.

What you learned was that your money was safe there, and that it was liquid. You could withdraw it when you wished. You weren't earning much on that bank savings account, but your rate of return was irrelevant. You were saving up for something you wanted to buy soon, and the bank kept your money secure.

3 Stages of Money

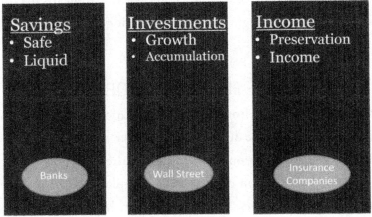

From there, as you entered the workforce, at some point you learned about a retirement account through your employer, whether it was a 401(k) or a 403-B or 457 or the like. That's when the world of Wall Street entered your life. This is the realm of brokers and money managers. That's when you focus on growth and accumulation. You learn that when you put money in such investments, sometimes your account goes up and sometimes it goes down. There is risk involved.

During those working years, a dip in the market wasn't a huge concern: What was important was that you continued to add to your account. As long as you had your job and your income, you didn't need that money. You were investing for the long term. While you didn't enjoy watching your savings go down, you could handle that because you didn't need to withdraw from your account for income to live on. You were able to handle that risk, and hopefully you still were adding to your portfolio. You focused on growth and savings and investments, and you took the risks and accumulated those assets. Your long-term goal was to eventually have the financial freedom to leave the workforce. You were on the path to financial security.

And when you are ready to retire, you need to focus on preserving what you have and using it to generate income. This is when you should be dealing with the third world of money: investments with insurance companies, in which you can create that income and do so securely.

Typically, then, the first financial experience people have is with banks. As they progress in their careers and accumulation years, they become involved in Wall Street investments. Then, when they need to generate income for retirement, they become involved in insurance vehicles.

MOVING FROM WORLD TO WORLD

As you move from world to world, it's not as simple as starting with bank savings, and then moving everything from that bucket into the Wall Street bucket, and later dumping it all into the insurance bucket. It's a far more sophisticated process than that. You need to make sure that you have the right money set aside in the right place for the right time.

It has always been a simple rule that once you attain financial security, you can begin to withdraw some of your money for income. The question is this: How much income do you need? In working with clients, I draw a line from the investment stage to the income stage and explain that they should move enough money to generate income to cover their essential expenses.

That is money for expenses that they simply must cover under any circumstances. That's the money that they move from Wall Street investments to insurance tools so that they can be assured of that income. They need to know that it will come in, regardless of what happens in the economy and the stock market.

During the 1980s and 1990s, Wall Street was telling retirees essentially this: "You don't have to move that money over there anymore. We're a lot smarter. We have better computer models. We have better investing strategies and products. We have better income planning strategies and asset diversification. You can leave your money here and take a 4 percent withdrawal rate and be okay."

As a result, many people didn't follow the basic rule, and they stayed in the investment phase. During the '80s and '90s, the market was going up, so they were fine. As long as you experience a bull market, you should be all right dealing with Wall Street. However, in the last decade, the market did not go up. Whether you call it a bear market or a long-term flat market, we saw a couple of big drops during that ten-year period, and the result, for many, was devastating.

One of the large wire houses did a study and found that in the year 2000, investors with a supposedly conservative mix of half stocks and half bonds and a 4 percent withdrawal rate could expect a 92 percent chance of success. Based on what happened in the economy during the ensuing decade, the average retiree following that advice, still taking that 4 percent withdrawal rate, experienced a 43 percent drop in portfolio value.

The difference is they were no longer adding to their accounts. They were still taking that 4 percent withdrawal rate. When the market went down, their portfolios went down even more because they had to take out that income. Those people pretty much know they're going to run out of money. That's the principle of dollar cost averaging working in reverse.

What that tells us is that you should follow Wall Street's advice only if you know you will experience a bull market throughout your retirement years. If you are not so certain, you need to move some money to generate the income that you will need. You need to identify how to appropriately allocate that money.

ONE COUPLE'S THREE SCENARIOS

A couple came into my office with $1.6 million in Wall Street investments. They were generating that conservative 4 percent withdrawal rate, which was $64,000 a year.

They were concerned about the economy and what would happen in a correction because they knew that not only would they experience losses but they would still have to pull out that same income. That would mean their percentage of withdrawal would be higher, 4.5 percent or 5 percent. They worried that their lifestyle would eventually suffer and that they eventually would run out of money. But if they kept the withdrawal rate at 4 percent, their income would be insufficient.

We worked with that couple to identify their options, and we looked at the three industries: the banks, Wall Street, and the insurers. With the low CD rates, we saw that in the banking industry, to generate their target of $64,000 a year, they would need to deposit $2.1 million into the bank.

They only had their $1.6 million, however, and with their Wall Street investments they were getting their $64,000 by withdrawing 4 percent. The problem, as they recognized, was that their income was not guaranteed. They would lose out when a correction came to the market.

When we looked at the third industry, insurance, they saw that basically for a $1 million deposit, they could generate their $64,000. Not only would that income be guaranteed, but that choice also freed up $600,000 that could be put to other uses now that it wasn't needed to generate their desired income. The couple opted to leave that money in Wall Street investments according to their risk comfort level. They could do so knowing that if they did experience losses on that $600,000, there would be no repercussions on their income.

In short, they used fewer dollars to produce the same income, guaranteed, and they now had plenty of additional money to invest. They still got their $64,000 every year, regardless of what happened in the economy, to add to their Social Security, pension, and their other income sources. They were in a much better position.

YOUR RISK COMFORT LEVEL

In retirement, people need to look at their risk exposure and make sure they feel they can handle it. That means they are investing according to their risk comfort level. And they must understand the risks that they truly are facing.

Remember the people's stories I outlined at the beginning of the book? This is where most of their plans went awry. They had no idea how much of their portfolios were at risk until the market corrected and they learned the hard way.

They believed their portfolios were conservative, and safe. (Trust me, "conservative" can mean something entirely different to a broker than it does to the average investor.) You need to know exactly how much of your assets are exposed to risk and what a loss would mean to your financial security in retirement. That's why, in my practice, we conduct a full global risk analysis of each of our client's assets.

In retirement, you must not lose the financial security that you worked so long to attain. Therefore you must identify what you truly need to spend and how much money you need to set aside to produce that income. That money then must be positioned to guarantee that income.

It's not about hitting a home run. It should be more about getting singles and doubles, meaning you need to consistently earn a fair rate of return. That means that in some years the market will go up more than you earned, but in other years when the market sinks, you don't sink with it; you still receive that consistent return. You eliminate the big swings of market volatility and you preserve your nest egg.

ONLY TAKE RISKS WITH YOUR RESERVES

It's not that you should avoid all risks. After setting aside the money you know you will need to produce retirement income for your needs and wants, you can take risks with your remaining assets, your reserves, but within reason.

You need to put the right money in the right place as time passes. Remember: Time at this stage in your life is not on your side. You need to identify how much money you need so you can retire with enough income. In the next chapter I will go into detail about income planning for retirement.

Let me clarify what I mean about time. When a lot of people hear that an investor needs time on his side, they think that means that because they are older, it's too late for them. But what it means is that they must decide when they will need their money. Whatever they need soon can be used to create some guaranteed income streams. The remainder still can be invested to grow with time. You have to categorize your money so that you do not take risks with the money you need immediately or soon. When you're going to need the money is what matters.

When you set up income buckets for your retirement, you know that you have guaranteed income to address your needs and your wants. The latter is money you may not be using, but you are glad it is there. It provides extra financial security, and you want to keep it secure.

After you have addressed those needs and wants, you can go further out in time and decide what to do with any remaining assets. You can take greater risks with that money because you are probably never going to need it. Now you've put time back on your side. If you make a bad investment, a bad decision, you do not need that money. You did not aggravate the situation and make it even worse. Let's take a look at some investment strategies.

QUALITY, DEPENDABLE INVESTMENTS

Wall Street says you should diversify between equities and fixed income, between stocks and bonds. But if you look back to 2008 and examine the portfolios of people who owned what was considered the best stocks, they still likely lost money. Back in the 1980s and 1990s, retirees could focus more on capital gains. Nowadays they should focus on yield: dividends, interest, investments that generate some type of yield to serve as income.

Quality of investment is of prime importance. The word *quality* in the financial sector is defined pretty much the same as it is anywhere else. If you shop for a car, you probably are looking for one that meets your needs and will be dependable. It's the same idea in the financial sector. You want quality that is dependable. What's the chance that the investment is going to perform as expected?

You also will want to ensure that your investments are diversified in the right sectors, not all sectors, but rather, the appropriate ones. In the recent economy, for example, many people looked for "defensive" investments that could weather the downturn. They considered the kind of businesses that would do well even in troubled times.

Your portfolio also should be diversified globally, with appropriate positions in world markets, and you may want to consider some investments outside the stock market itself, such as alternative investments.

When a portfolio is designed to hit such doubles and singles instead of home runs, the volatility can be tamed, and that helps to preserve your principal. The key is to preserve that principal while still earning a fair rate of return. In 2008 Wall Street tried to reassure people that we were all in the same sinking boat. Wall Street often tries to send out that message, and it is false. Our clients, using the strategies that I am advocating, preserved their principal and earned a fair rate of return. That is possible for people who have first set aside enough of their assets in safe income-producing vehicles so that they know they won't run out of money. Then, with the remaining assets, they can invest, and if they do it right, they won't lose money even when the sky is falling for others.

People make rash decisions when they think the sky is falling. They search for the high returns that they think are their key to survival, and as a result, we have seen a huge push toward junk bonds. Investors are basically giving money to a company or corporation with crummy credit. The risk is great, and in retirement it should be unacceptable.

BONDS WILL BE HURTING

For many years it was easy to make money in the bond market. As interest rates were dropping and new bonds had ever lower rates, the older ones in your portfolio that paid higher rates gained in value.

In such a low-interest-rate environment, when the interest rates do rise, you're going to see people who are harmed in their bond portfolios. It will work in reverse: As the newer bonds pay a higher rate, who will want your old bonds that pay less? You can expect a loss—it almost seems guaranteed—and how many years will it take just to get back to breakeven?

In that kind of environment, bonds are going to be fraught with many problems and surprises, as people lose more than they imagined they could. They would be wise to look for other kinds of yields with a fair—and safer—return.

IF NOT THE STOCK MARKET, WHERE?

The major financial firm of Putnam Investments is headquartered in Boston, but businesswise it is Wall Street all the way. Even so, Putnam was recommending in a 2011 report that retirees should restrict their stock market investments to only 5 to 25 percent of their portfolios if their goal is to sustain their withdrawals and avoid running out of money.

The point is that even Wall Street knows you shouldn't invest very much of your retirement money in the stock market. The question remains, however, "If not there, where?"

Creating a Secure Retirement Income

"Chris, I'm getting older," the man explained as he and his wife met with me in my office. "I don't want to go back to work again. I want to stop this. I'm looking for something better." I hear such pleas all the time, but this couple's tale was particularly saddening.

He had retired in 1998, and they had moved to a lovely area just off Lake Tahoe and started to withdraw income from their portfolio. Along came the market correction of 2001, and they lost too much. So he returned to work for another five years. He was living down in Los Angeles while his wife stayed back home. Finally, his portfolio was back to where it had been, and he retired again, and along came the economic storm of 2008. And it's back to work for another stretch in L.A.

Now he's back, trying once again to retire. That's fourteen years of frustrations, during which he retired three times. "Hang in there," his broker kept telling him. "Just go back to work for a while, and the market will come back." But after all those years, he has no gain to show for the added work. He just kept battling back to even, and if you factor in inflation, this couple has actually suffered quite a loss.

The couple has friends who were clients of mine and who lost nothing in the last market correction. Their portfolios still grew, they had a good income, and they didn't have to go back to work. "That's what we want," the man told me. "What's different? What are they doing that we're not doing?"

IN SEARCH OF ANSWERS

How can you guarantee that you'll have secure retirement income that lasts the rest of your life now that the old three-legged stool is broken? You can't count on Wall Street, so what is the answer?

Financial Planning Rule of Thumb

Income	Age-Based	Current
	100	
82%	-60% Safe	27%
18%	40% Risk	73%

Here is how the traditional "Rule of 100" works (or doesn't, as the case may be): Start with 100 and subtract your age. If you're 60 years old, for example, start with 100 and subtract 60. The result is 40. That means, as a rule of thumb, that 60 percent of your assets should be in safe investments, and up to

40 percent can be in riskier investments. If you are 70 years old, your financial planning rule of thumb would be to put 70 percent in safe investments and up to 30 percent in riskier investments, and so on.

The reason for this? As we have discussed, the older you are, the less time you have to recover from losses. But take caution: The amount of risk that the Rule of 100 suggests would be appropriate might not be suitable for you at all.

I recently met with a married couple, both 65 years old and recently retired. They had been told that their portfolio was conservative, but we identified that, in fact, they had 73 percent at risk and just 27 percent was safe. Their risk exposure exceeded their risk comfort level. But even more importantly, they needed to identify how much risk, or loss, their portfolio could handle without affecting their retirement income.

After weighing their savings amount against their lifestyle goals and life expectancies, we established that for stable income throughout their retirement years, they would need 82 percent of their assets in safe investments and only up to 18 percent at risk. In other words, if they were to lose more than 18 percent of their assets, they would either have to change their lifestyle or risk running out of money.

Note that there are two types of losses we're dealing with here: The first is how much loss you feel is acceptable, your risk comfort level. The second is how much you can lose before your financial security, or simply put, your lifestyle, is jeopardized. That's called your income loss cap. Ask yourself at what point you would feel poor.

WILL YOUR MONEY LAST?

A recent study by T. Rowe Price said there's an 89 percent chance of having your money last as long as you do when using a traditional retirement planning approach, for example, investing in stocks, bonds, mutual funds, exchange-traded funds (ETFs), and so on.

Are you okay with an 89 percent chance of success? At the end of 2010, after the ravages of the recession, that chance of success with the traditional approach was only 29 percent.

Let me help put that in context. You're sitting in a plane about to fly to Hawaii for a nice vacation. Before the flight attendant closes the door, the pilot announces that after mapping the route he has identified that you'll be flying through a storm. He feels confident everything will be all right, though, because based on prior experience there's an 89 percent chance that the plane will arrive safely at the destination. In other words, there's an 11 percent chance that the plane will crash into the ocean.

What would you do? Stay on the plane and hope for the best, or exit the plane now and find a better option?

A BETTER WAY

I hope I have made this point quite clear: The amount of money that you need for generating income should be invested in absolutely safe accounts. If you have a reserve beyond that, you can invest it based on your risk comfort level if you choose, but you must not rely on Wall Street investments for steady income in retirement. Those accounts can generate 3 percent to 4 percent a year for withdrawals, but it's not guaranteed. We call this "maybe income." (Remember that "89 percent chance of success" that didn't turn out so well?) The brokerage industry thinks this is good enough for retirees, but I disagree. You deserve better. You deserve a secure retirement, regardless of which way the market is going.

What, then, is an alternative? Insurance products are designed to generate income. They can provide a 5 percent to 7 percent annual payout. This is contractually guaranteed monthly income for the rest of your life, no matter what the markets do.

Put your money in the right place, and do it at the right time. Don't wait until the day you retire to start shifting money from investment accounts to income accounts, especially in markets such as these. In my experience with difficult economies, people tend to look at this not in the last five years of their working career, but in the last ten. Just look at what happened in the last decade and you'll see why this makes sense. The people who began shifting their money over sooner rather than later were nicely rewarded with fewer losses, greater returns, and increased financial security.

SEQUENTIAL INCOME PLANNING (SIP) STRATEGIES

Sequential income planning strategies let you know how much income you can generate from your investments so that you can be assured of enough money to cover your needs for the rest of your life. At the same time, you can be insulated from market losses, the effects of inflation, and the costs of long-term care. You know where your income is coming from now and for the long term.

A sequential income plan should address four main concerns that a retiree will have:

- A guaranteed income. You can know that you will have that income regardless of what the economy or the markets throw at you.

- A hedge against inflation. Your income will adjust as time goes by so that you maintain your spending power.

- Long-term-care protection. You can be prepared for a possible long-term illness and the accompanying increased costs of care.

- Flexibility. You will be able to adjust if and when your circumstances change.

The SIP typically is set up with four "legs" or positions for your money. Let's take a look at each.

Leg 1

Your first leg is money that you are going to generate now. It will produce income for up to three years. What you need for this leg would typically be cash—money in bank savings, for example—to deal with your needs for now and the short term, measured in months or a few years.

Leg 2

When the money in that first leg has all been spent, that's when Leg 2 comes into play. You had set this one up for your intermediate or mid-term income needs, for example, to generate an income for the third through tenth year of your retirement, though the time periods vary from person to person. Typically, the income from Leg 2 is from some type of annuity. You have guaranteed yourself that income, figuring exactly how much to invest in that leg to produce the needed income for that period. You don't want any surprises.

Leg 3

Leg 3 is your long-term income, starting typically about the eleventh year and continuing for as long as you or your spouse is still alive. You begin to receive that after the money in the second leg runs out. One product that works well for the investment in this third leg is typically what's known as a hybrid income annuity, with a guaranteed income rider. That means that you would have an income account that would compound, let's say, by 5 to 8 percent each year, and that's a given. You know exactly how much you need to invest to generate "x" amount of income, guaranteed, from the eleventh year and for the rest of your life. It's also important to look into getting a bonus: a long-term-care rider. Some hybrid income annuities double your income to help pay for a long-term illness and associated expenses. That may save you from having to spend money for premiums for traditional long-term-care insurance.

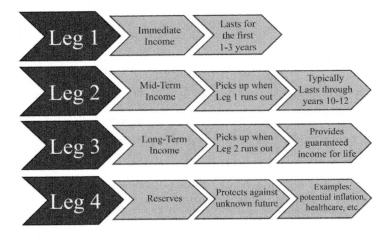

Leg 4

The first three legs, then, generate your income for the rest of your life. The fourth leg becomes your reserves. That's the money that you don't need for generating retirement income. That's the money that you typically will invest in the world of Wall Street, according to your risk comfort level. That money could be for a further hedge against inflation, perhaps more inflation than your plan anticipates. Or maybe it's for additional health care, or for travel. It could be to purchase a new car, or to leave a legacy. For whatever purpose, your investments will be in place to fulfill them.

So long as you develop those first three legs appropriately, according to your sequential income plan, the fourth leg can be money placed in investments that incur risk. How much risk you can accept will be unique to you, depending on your personal and family situation, and your stomach for what can happen on Wall Street. Some people say, "I don't want to take any risk in the market," and that's fine. Other people say that since they have "x" amount in conservative investments, they therefore can accept more risk with another portion of their money.

In that way, your SIP has flexibility built into it, and it also builds confidence. You know that you're going to be all right, that you're going to have enough money to last throughout your retirement no matter what happens. You generate safe, secure income for the rest of your life.

This needs to be accomplished with care, of course. You don't want the kind of annuity in which you lose control of the money so that you get a payout, but when you die, the insurance company keeps whatever is left. I've never had anyone come into my office and tell me, "I want to name the insurance company as my beneficiary."

Instead, you need to structure the SIP and put the right strategies in place for each leg, and then you need to increase your payout rate to 6 or 6.5 percent or more. You must be able to adjust for inflation, and your income for the first three legs must be guaranteed. You need it to cover your nondiscretionary expenses—for example, putting food on the table, and covering utilities, insurance, and health-care costs. No matter what happens, you still need income to cover those expenses.

As you can see, a well-designed SIP is an efficient way to maximize income with as few dollars as possible, and to have that income 100 percent guaranteed. If the economy takes a downturn, and we see a correction in the market, that income is not lost. The SIP can, in fact, ensure that inflation will never overcome you, and certainly the handwriting is on the wall that we all will have to be dealing with that threat. That protection too can be built into the plan so that you can sleep well, knowing that you will not run out of money.

Once your strategy is in place, you will have a clear vision for your future. Knowing that your needs are covered, you gain flexibility. You can enjoy your retirement. Your income provides for your lifestyle and the kind of life you desire. Lose the income, and you lose the life. But if that income is guaranteed, you will know the money is there not only for emergencies and contingencies but to make your retirement everything that you dreamed it could be.

CHAPTER 9

Healthy Pursuits

There are some things that we just don't like to think about, being struck by a debilitating disease, for example, or having a spouse die. Unfortunately, ignoring such possibilities doesn't make them go away. In fact, it sets you and your loved ones up for an even worse scenario should catastrophe strike.

A retired couple recently came to see me for advice. They had been through the 2008 market correction but had continued withdrawing the 4 percent from their investments that they had been told would be a good bet. Their broker had told them to just hang in there and the market would come back.

When the market did come back, though, they couldn't make it back to breakeven because of those withdrawals they had needed for income. And they hadn't wanted to spend money on long-term-care insurance, reasoning that they probably wouldn't need it anyway, and even if they did, their investments ought to be enough to cover that cost.

Not only did they lose too much money in the market, but they also soon found themselves facing another huge challenge:

the husband developed dementia. The wife did what she could to take care of him at home as she watched their portfolio get ever smaller. In time, the caretaking became too much for her. She admitted him to a long-term-care facility that specialized in care for dementia, which typically is more expensive. But by that time, their portfolio was not the size that they had imagined it would be for such a contingency. It has, in fact, never rebounded, and the expenses have continued, not only for the long-term care but for all other expenses involved in maintaining a household.

"We have a problem," she told me when they came to my office, and that was clear enough. The problem was exacerbated by the fact that some of her husband's pension and Social Security would stop when he passed away. She would need even greater income from the investments than they needed in their earlier years. Their portfolio was getting ever smaller, even as she was taking less income, she was trying to make ends meet under the multiple pressures of inflation, medical costs, rising property taxes, and more, not the least of which was the cost of the long-term care.

She was looking for a plan. Obviously she wanted to be able to cover his nursing home expenses, and she also wanted enough money remaining after he died to last for her own lifetime and to replace the lost pension and Social Security benefits. He eventually did pass away, and her plan became "moving to a new neighborhood." She had to sell their home at a time when the real estate market was down. She moved to a less expensive home across town, which also tended to isolate her from friends. Her lifestyle changed.

None of that had to be. If that couple had simply planned more efficiently for their future, the scenario would have turned out to be much more pleasant. They should have assessed whether the money they had saved would be sufficient and positioned it so that it wouldn't be swallowed by a market correction. They should have made dependable plans for some kind of long-term care, and they should have anticipated and planned for how they would replace the income if one of them were to die.

IT COULD HAPPEN TO YOU AND YOUR FAMILY

Many people do not imagine that it could happen to them. They must ask the hard questions: 1) "Am I at risk of losing more than I can afford to lose if the market sinks?" 2) "Do I have any plan to pay for long-term care, if that need should arise?" and 3) "How much income will we lose if one of us passes away, and how can that be replaced?"

If you do need to go into a facility, be aware that some states have filial responsibility laws that allow the state or the long-term-care facility to collect debts for long-term care. Some states even are authorized to go after the children to collect on that debt. We've been seeing cases in which they have succeeded in forcing the children to pay. It hasn't been happening in great numbers, but one must wonder whether such actions will increase as states feel the increasing pressure of more people on Medicaid and increasing health-care costs. As money to fill the gaps is diminishing on the state level, the question is whether more states will look toward enforcing filial responsibility laws. Time will certainly tell.

How many people are really willing to transfer that burden to their children? Too often, the children are dealing with aging parents and at the same time looking to send their own children through college. Most people would never want to visit such a hardship on their loved ones.

Do yourself and your family a favor by realistically planning now for how you will replace any income lost due to the death of a spouse, and how you will produce the income needed in case of long-term illness.

LONG-TERM-CARE OPTIONS

One in two Americans over the age of 65 today faces some type of long-term-care scenario. That could be the need for in-home care, assisted living, or skilled nursing care. Whatever the case, you should plan for some increase in future expenses related to health care.

If you are like many people, you may be harboring two false beliefs about how you will afford long-term care. Let me disillusion you of those. First, Medicare is not going to take care of your long-term-care issues. It is unlikely that you will be able to jump through the hoops required in order to get a very limited benefit for a very limited time. And second, Medicaid is not your answer. To qualify for Medicaid, you have to be financially destitute.

Where does that leave you? There are several options, including:

Free long-term-care benefits. Believe it or not, some free long-term-care benefits are available. If you're a veteran who served during wartime, for example, you may be able to get help for your long-term-care needs, either at home or in a US Department of Veterans Affairs (VA) facility. Such free benefits may only supplement other long-term-care options. However, it's certainly worthwhile to be aware of any free benefits for which you may be eligible.

Long-term-care insurance. Traditional long-term-care insurance is relatively pricey, and the cost can seem especially daunting when there's a chance, however slim, that you won't need the coverage for which you spent all that money on premiums. Not everyone can qualify for long-term-care insurance, and many of those who do qualify choose not to buy it because of the expense. Nonetheless, in many cases it's the wisest choice among the options available. Be sure that your plan provides for an increase, typically 5 percent each year, to cover inflation. Also, be aware that insurers can certainly increase premiums, and you may face restrictions such as a delay before coverage takes effect.

Self-Insuring. That means having enough money in your savings to cover long-term care if the need for it arises. This is an option for relatively wealthy people. Going back to the three buckets we talked about in Chapter 6, the second one, which contains your "later" money, would be the place to plan for this contingency. If long-term care becomes necessary, you would "turn on the spigot" to make money available to cover the costs of care. You do not want the money that you have set aside for long-term care to be subjected to significant market risk, although you do need enough of a return to keep up with the increasing costs of care.

Putting the burden on someone else. I will list this as an option, but let me again emphasize that you should think long and hard about this. Do you really want to put family members or others in the position of caring for you themselves, paying for your care, or both? Your spouse may very well need care too. And your children will most likely be stretched to meet their own career, family, and financial obligations as well as planning for their own retirement. Granted, it works in some situations, but I would hesitate to rely on this as your only option.

Investment vehicles with a rider for long-term illness or an accelerated death benefit. This is often the best choice for people who don't qualify for traditional long-term-care insurance. A variety of income vehicles provide double benefits if the owner is stricken with a long-term illness, for example. Some life insurance policies have an accelerated death benefit rider, meaning that the death benefit can be converted to cover long-term care if it is needed, but if left unused, it's passed on tax-free to heirs. Many times retirees wonder whether they still need their life insurance, but often the best move is to upgrade it, as you would a cell phone or computer, when better products become available, such as those that provide for long-term care. If you already have some life insurance, you could look into converting it to one of those types. That's a way to acquire the protection you need while controlling your costs.

YOUR UNIQUE CIRCUMSTANCES

You may be thinking, "Chris, it's too late for me. I should have done that back in my 40s or 50s. I don't think I could get it now." But most people are not addressing this issue in their 40s or 50s. Most people are addressing this issue when they're planning for retirement. They then may run out and meet with a long-term-care insurance salesman, and there is nothing wrong with this, but you're only looking at one particular product.

It is far better to meet with a financial adviser who can help identify which options or strategies make the most sense for you and are worth pursuing. The best strategy depends in large part on your personal and family situation. It depends on your physical condition as well as your financial condition.

Every person's situation is unique. A woman came to see me who had enough income and assets in a form that if she had a long-term illness, her lifestyle would not change. Also, if she were to go into a long-term-care facility, the home could also be sold and the equity also would cover expenses. We identified that she really didn't need long-term-care insurance because she had enough income and assets that could be converted for income, and she didn't have children to whom she was leaving money.

On the other hand, long-term-care insurance certainly makes sense for many single people. Without a spouse who might be relied upon to provide some care and support, that person has a greater chance of needing to enter a long-term-care facility. And for married couples, the insurance need can be particularly crucial. If the husband, for example, develops a long-term illness, the income needs to increase to pay for the care. If he passes away and income is lost, it needs to be replaced.

In my practice, I dedicate a significant amount of time, though just part of the retirement planning process, to long-term-care planning and identifying issues that need to be addressed—which assets are at risk, for example—and how to protect against a spend-down for Medicaid assistance. I explore each client's various long-term-care options and put a plan in place to identify the best solution. I have seen many people like you and worked with many retirees and understand what they are facing. Long-term care is a universal concern among retirees, and solutions await you.

Your Mark on the World

What does "legacy planning" mean to you? Writing a will? Establishing a trust? Naming your power of attorney? Yes, legal documentation is certainly an important part of legacy planning, but it can be a lot more complex than that. I like to think of it as a Venn diagram with one circle for legal planning and the other for financial planning. In this chapter I'll highlight some of the most important elements in the area where the two circles intersect.

IS YOUR POWER OF ATTORNEY POWERLESS?

A power of attorney (POA) is a supporting document to your will or trust. Do you have one? If so, have you read it? It's a particularly critical document if you should ever become incapacitated and unable to manage your affairs. I urge you to pay attention to it now and make sure it spells out your wishes fully and accurately.

In the document, you appoint an agent to make decisions about your financial affairs. Many attorneys include language restricting the amount of money that can be "gifted" from your accounts. This is to prevent agents from making excessive gifts to themselves or others. The IRS annual gift exclusion rule allows people to give up to a certain amount per year, per person, without it being counted toward their one-time, lifetime gifting exclusion amount. In 2013 the annual gift exclusion amount was $14,000.

Though inserted for your protection, the POA language can cause you to lose assets you might need if a long-term disability occurs that requires skilled nursing care, assets that could be protected if the POA were drafted differently.

Example: After Martin suffered a severe stroke, he was moved to a long-term-care facility. His wife, Irene, had power of attorney and was also the beneficiary of his $300,000 IRA. Because his POA document included language limiting the "gifting" amount, Irene was only able to access $14,000 from Martin's account, which was barely enough to pay for his first two months at the nursing home. Her only alternative was to go through the Medicaid spend-down process, whereby money from his IRA would go directly to the nursing home. Is this what Martin really wanted? To avoid situations like that, it is important to work with an advisor who understands those issues and can make sure there is true power in your power of attorney.

REVOCABLE LIVING TRUSTS

A revocable living trust is often used as an alternative to a will. It circumvents the need for probate and enables you to maintain control of your assets while you're living, and to specifically direct your successor, or "trustee," with regard to the distribution of your assets after your incapacity and/or death.

In the spirit of full disclosure, let me point out again that my father wrote the book on revocable living trusts. Really, he did. I highly recommend *The Living Trust* if you want to know more about this simple, inexpensive legal alternative that eliminates the costs and delays of probate and ensures that your loved ones receive their inheritance promptly and exactly as you intended.

A revocable living trust does have its limitations. It doesn't help you reduce your taxes or increase your retirement income, for example. It doesn't protect you from the expenses associated with long-term care. In my experience, by simply creating a revocable living trust and ignoring the rest, chances are your estate won't be large enough to even warrant a trust at death.

Still, it's not that hard to establish a good trust these days. The real value comes when it's time to settle the trust. When someone passes away, where do the heirs usually go to have the estate settled? Back to the attorney who drafted the will and/or trust. The attorney is typically best suited for dealing with the legal aspects of settling the trust, but what about the tax and financial issues?

A financial advisor who specializes in retirement planning can help you set up your trust with an eye toward your exit strategy.

TAX-EFFICIENT DISTRIBUTION

Once you have decided who will inherit the assets that remain upon your death, it's important to make sure that they will be distributed in the most tax-efficient manner.

I discussed one such consideration in Chapter 6: Some IRA accounts can be structured to "stretch" the money that remains at your death over the lifetimes of your children and grandchildren. Rather than inheriting all of the money at once—and paying tax on it—your heirs can receive a portion of it each year (in the form of a required minimum distribution), as long as they live. Taxes are significantly reduced since the taxable amount is limited to the annual distributions. Moreover, the money that remains in the account continues to grow, tax-deferred.

Another major consideration is which assets should be left to charity. That's an important part of leaving a legacy, but many times people end up leaving the wrong type or the wrong assets to charity, and that just creates an additional tax burden on whatever is left to their family, usually the children or grandchildren.

A mistake I see many times is when people leave money in retirement accounts, or annuities, to their family. These are not always the most tax efficient assets to pass on. The assets that are subject to the highest taxes, such as money from a retirement account, are the ones that should go to charity because when a charity receives such assets, it pays no tax. That allows you to leave more behind with less going to the government. You can leave other assets to your family and noncharity heirs, and those should be your tax-free investments or those that are subject to less taxation.

CHARITABLE CONSIDERATIONS

If you list a charity as a beneficiary of your retirement accounts, you can create an immediate taxable distribution on all of the money inside that retirement account when you pass away. You want to make sure that it's done properly so that you don't create an adverse tax consequence.

Also, many times people tell their estate planning attorney that they want to leave a certain percentage to charity, and the attorney drafts that language into the trust. The problem is that the trust doesn't control the distribution of retirement accounts. It does control the distribution of your other assets, however, some of which are tax-free and tax efficient and therefore should go to family and noncharity heirs. Because of the language, however, some of those assets go to charity. Meanwhile, the retirement account will then typically go to the children, and they will face a heavy tax on it, whereas a charity would have paid no tax on the bequest. You want to make sure that the trust is truly set up properly and doesn't merely state a percentage that will go to charity. If you do that, you are leaving the wrong assets to charity. It's an extremely important consideration that is missed far too many times, resulting in unnecessary taxation to heirs.

ESTATE-TAX EXEMPTION

It's important to be sure that you're making the most of estate tax exemptions. What most people also miss is that many times upon death, when the spouse directly inherits the retirement account, it cannot be used to fund the estate-tax exemption. What often happens as a result is that the deceased's estate-tax exemption is lost. Therefore, when the surviving spouse dies, he or she ends up paying estate taxes that could have been avoided simply through better planning when the first spouse died. Proper funding of subtrusts can keep the exemptions intact, and that's another huge issue in estate planning that often is entirely missed.

WILLS VERSUS TRUSTS

A will typically guarantees that you go through probate, the legal process of establishing its validity. A trust is designed to avoid probate, which is expensive, can tie up assets for months, and opens your affairs to the public. By comparison, setting up a trust saves both time and money and reduces the tax bite.

Not everyone needs a trust. You may be able to eliminate the need to create a living trust if you don't own real estate and you typically own assets that can bypass probate, ones with a named beneficiary such as life insurance, a retirement account, a brokerage account, or a checking or savings account where you can have a POD or TOD (payable on death or transfer on death). But most people will need a trust to avoid probate.

A trust allows you to maintain control of your money even after you're gone. While you're alive, a trust typically does not give you any asset protection, but if you have what's known as an A-B trust, when one spouse passes away, the assets that are placed in the B trust can be protected from any creditors in the future, such as litigants in a lawsuit.

Trusts can also be used as part of long-term-care planning. Those people who have not set up some type of long-term-care plan can leave their money to the surviving spouse in the B trust when they pass away. Whatever is in the B trust can be protected from the costs of long-term illness. In other words, that money would not have to be spent down before qualifying for Medicaid. It is important to incorporate the appropriate language inside the trust and the powers of attorney to allow the successor to be able to do what's known as Medicaid planning to protect, or exempt, or shelter assets so that they are not subjected to the spend-down.

A trust can also be designed to protect the assets from somebody you just don't like, such as a son-in-law who you feel has mistreated your daughter and would mistreat an inheritance, or to block him off if a divorce seems imminent. You can put the right language in a trust to protect the asset, or assets, for your child so that the in-law can have no part of it. You should keep the money for the beneficiary inside the trust, allowing your child to make withdrawals as needed and be able to leave the rest protected.

A trust can also protect retirement accounts. Typically, if you simply list your children as beneficiaries, they bring that money into their own estates, and then it's subjected to their own and also their spouse's creditors, lawsuits, judgments, liens, divorces—those types of things. However, you need to use proper planning. You typically do not want to list your living trust as the beneficiary of your retirement accounts. If you do that, when you pass away, all of that money likely will become immediately 100 percent taxable. That's similar to the tax nightmare of putting the kids in a higher tax bracket. Those are some advanced planning issues, but it pays to know about them.

With a trust, you can do pretty much anything you want in distributing those assets to your children or others over time. If you have a child who isn't too good with money, you can certainly specify that a sum left to that child will be distributed as income over the rest of his or her life. The right type of financial product can be used to generate that lifetime income without having to keep the trust open and deal with trust administration.

You will need to make sure that your trust documents establish that the people whom you will put in charge if you can't make your own financial or medical decisions will have the power and ability to do planning at that time on your behalf. You do not necessarily have to go out and do all the planning for something that may or may not happen, but you do need to have language in your trust giving the authority to take appropriate action. You don't want to hamstring your beneficiaries.

ENVISIONING A LEGACY

I find that people often are hesitant to address their estate planning issues because they're still concerned about their own financial security. Until they can feel comfortable about that, it's hard to do more.

Once they have addressed those issues, once they have created a plan for financial security, and have an income strategy that reassures them that they're going to be okay, they can envision what they want to leave behind as a legacy, and what that would look like. That's when estate planning can truly begin.

As people reach their retirement age and beyond, their thoughts often turn to whom and what matters most to them. When they discover that they have the financial capacity to do more than take care of themselves, they gain a sense of freedom that allows them to finally consider how they will make their mark on the world.

Where Do We Go from Here?

The average person spends much of his or her lifetime building financial security, but it can be lost, never to be regained. That's why you need to carefully assess your definition of financial security and make sure it is realistic for the goals that you have set. You can take the necessary steps to put that plan in place, and never lose that financial security, and to pass on your values and assets to the coming generations.

Retirement planning is designed to create peace of mind. If you're on vacation, you don't have to be watching the market or worried about what happened in the economy and how that might affect you. If you are taking any investment risks, they are appropriate ones and you are comfortable with them. You have learned the questions to ask and the problems to solve before moving forward to make wise decisions.

You can count yourself a success when you can put your head on the pillow for a good night's sleep, knowing that you have identified and dealt with all your financial challenges. You can live the lifestyle that you want and that you have earned. You can enjoy your retirement without having to always look over your shoulder for whatever threat might pop up and derail your plans.

Study after study shows that retirement is the time when most people change advisors. As they get close to that stage, they switch to one who specializes in retirement planning to put the right strategies in place. The reason is clear: This is a different time of life. What once was good advice may be very bad advice now.

Things change, not only in one's life but also in the economy and on the political scene, and it pays to be aware. Is the foundation of your financial house secure, with an income that is guaranteed? Have you built solid walls, investing appropriately, and keeping inflation at bay? Are you living under a reliable roof, with assets positioned to grow? Is your house insulated and sturdy, safe from any economic storm?

You want to set the right example for your heirs and future generations. What are those people going to say about you? Did you make a difference in this life? Was your legacy more than money? Did you leave your values for posterity?

I know I have succeeded with my clients when they come to see me and the weight of the world no longer seems to be on their shoulders, regardless of what's happening in the economy, or in the market, or in Washington. They appear to have not a care in the world. They have come to talk about finances, but they seem more interested in showing me pictures of the grandchildren, or of their latest vacation.

In short, they are enjoying this season of life. That's what it's all about. Often when I first meet clients, they have a drawn look on their faces as if worn down by worry. Now those lines of worry have lifted. They have succeeded in redefining their retirement.

ABOUT THE AUTHOR

Christopher K. Abts, is the President of Cornerstone Retirement Group, a company specializing in comprehensive retirement planning strategies for individuals, private business owners, and physicians. He primarily focuses in retirement planning, wealth preservation and estate planning and has helped hundreds of clients prepare for retirement through his proprietary planning process.

Chris is a Registered Investment Advisor, licensed insurance agent, and holds a Series 65. He is a Chartered Retirement Planning Counselor through the College for Financial Planning, a Certified Estate Planner through the National Institute of Estate Planning and he is a member of the National Association of Insurance and Financial Advisors.

Chris is the author of *Redefining Retirement* and routinely sought after by national and local media. As a financial guest commentator, he has appeared on CNBC, Fox News, *The Wall Street Journal, Smart Money Magazine,* Yahoo Finance, and TheStreet.com. Chris is regularly featured on Channel 2 News *Money Watch* and currently hosts a weekly retirement radio show in the northern Nevada area. *Senior Market Advisor Magazine* named him one of the Top 5 Retirement advisors in the nation.

Chris, his wife Julia, and their three children reside in Reno, Nevada.

Cornerstone Retirement Group

5525 Kietzke Lane, Suite 100

Reno, Nevada 89511

775-853-9033

www.CornerstoneRetirement.com

info@CornerstoneRetirement.com

CPSIA information can be obtained at www.ICGtesting.com
Printed in the USA
BVOW09s1820191114

375850BV00041B/959/P

9 781599 323381